Fairholt Frederick William

Homes, Haunts and Works of Rubens, Vandyke, Rembrandt and Cuyp

the Dutch genre-pa nters - Michael Angelo and Raffaelle. Being a series of

art-rambles in Eelgium, Holland and Italy

Fairholt Frederick William

Homes, Haunts and Works of Rubens, Vandyke, Rembrandt and Cuyp
the Dutch genre-painters - Michael Angelo and Raffaelle. Being a series of art-rambles in Belgium, Holland and Italy

ISBN/EAN: 9783337320942

Printed in Europe, USA, Canada, Australia, Japan

Cover: Foto ©Thomas Meinert / pixelio.de

More available books at **www.hansebooks.com**

THE VILLAGE ALEHOUSE.

From a Painting by Adrian van Ostade.

HOMES, HAUNTS, AND WORKS

OF

RUBENS, VANDYKE, REMBRANDT, AND CUYP;

THE DUTCH GENRE-PAINTERS;

MICHAEL ANGELO AND RAFFAELLE.

BEING

A Series of Art=Rambles

IN BELGIUM, HOLLAND, AND ITALY.

BY FREDERICK WILLIAM FAIRHOLT, F.S.A.,
AUTHOR OF "DICTIONARY OF TERMS IN ART," ETC.

Illustrated with One Hundred and Thirty-three Wood-engravings

NEW YORK:
D. APPLETON AND CO., BROADWAY.
1872.

PREFACE.

—◆—

RARELY are to be found combined in one individual the qualifications of the literary man, the artist, and the archæologist. The last may be able to use both pen and pencil, yet the latter only in such a way as to entitle him to the character of an antiquarian draughtsman; while the artist or the painter may have a literary taste, though it is seldom called into action; and he may also have arrived at such an amount of archæological attainment as will enable him to bring it to bear upon his art, but not beyond it. In the late F. W. FAIRHOLT, however, these three accomplishments showed themselves in a very remarkable manner. He certainly does not come under the denomination of a painter, for we do not think he ever used a brush and colour since his early days when he began life as a scene-painter, except, perhaps, in making a few sketches as *memoranda*; yet the black-lead pencil in his hand was an instrument employed to good and profitable purpose in an infinite variety of ways—landscapes, buildings, figure-subjects, and ornamental objects of every kind; and it was remarkable for accuracy in all his delineations from nature. His art was essentially realistic, induced mainly by working much on antiquarian objects, which require the utmost exactitude; its aim was truthfulness, and to this he sacrificed whatever mere fancy may have suggested in the way of rendering his subjects more picturesque. His eye and his hand were so accurate from long practice that we have known him to make an engraving—of a coin, for example—with his etching-needle on a plate, without first tracing its outline on the metal.

Either for pleasure, for health, or for literary and artistic purposes, he frequently visited the Continent; selecting, generally, those countries which he could most advantageously lay under contribution for the joint action of pen and pencil—places peculiarly attractive to the artist and antiquarian, either from their historic interest, and their picturesque character, or as the residence of those whose names are enrolled among the great painters and sculptors of the world. The Low Countries, and some of the old cities of Germany, such as Nuremberg, were his favourite localities for a month's ramble, and he would come back from them with a multitude of characteristic sketches of what he saw, and with his note-book well stored with intelligent comment, the result of active research and judicious investigation. Italy was, perhaps, less attractive to him than other parts of the Continent, for his artistic sympathies were more in harmony with the Gothic style of art, especially as regards architecture and all its associations, than with the Classic; yet in Rome and other Italian cities he found much to engage both mind and hand.

From materials gathered in different visits to these countries, he contributed, at various time, a number of papers to the pages of the *Art-Journal*, which, from the interesting character of the respective narratives, and the graphic illustrations from his own pencil that accompanied them, excited much interest at the period of their publication. In a collective form they cannot fail to be as attractive as when they appeared at intervals, if, indeed, they will not be found even more so. They are abundantly diversified in subject; art and artists, architecture, scenery, men and customs, each finding a niche more or less capacious in the literary and pictorial temple. In submitting this volume to the public, the publishers feel assured they are offering a work of pleasant and instructive reading; one, moreover, that may serve as a kind of "guide" to those who shall hereafter visit the localities of which it speaks.

J. D.

April, 1871.

CONTENTS.

THE HOUSE OF MICHAEL ANGELO, AT FLORENCE.

RAFFAELLE IN ROME.

LIST OF ILLUSTRATIONS.

— ·—

HOMES, HAUNTS, AND WORKS OF RUBENS AND HIS SCHOLARS.

HOMES, HAUNTS, AND WORKS OF RUBENS AND HIS SCHOLARS.

IN the old city of Cologne, hallowed by memories which come to us in unbroken succession from the days of the Romans, there arrived, to pass the last few years of life, the father of one destined to rank among the noblest masters of art. John Rubens, a man of learning and integrity, had held honourable office in his native city of Antwerp, where he had married Maria Pypelink, a scion of an old-established family there. But peace had fled from the Low Countries in the sanguinary wars which commenced between the Catholic and Protestant factions, and internecine war raged in the old city on the Scheldt. The Reformers, goaded to madness by the arrogance and determined cruelties of Spanish papal rule, rose *en masse*, and destroyed the monasteries and churches, burning and wasting the noble pictures and rich furniture of the altars, smashing the glorious windows of the sacred buildings, and defacing them within and without. These buildings, once the glory of Antwerp, were ruined in one night. The Catholic families fled from a city where the emperor's power could not suffice for their protection, and among the number were the parents of Rubens. They had descended from a Styrian family. Bartholomew Rubens, the father of John,

had first visited Brussels in attendance on the court of the
Emperor Charles V. in 1520 ; had married a Flemish lady of noble

Pet. Paul Rubens

birth, and then settled in Antwerp. His son fled from the city in
1566, and sought a home in the ancient city of Cologne. The

house he inhabited is still pointed out to the visitor,—it is in the
"Sternen Gasse," No. 10; but in that city of tortuous narrow
lanes the stranger may walk wearily and far in a futile attempt to
find it without a competent guide. The tall houses, the narrow
streets, and the tendency of the latter to wind suddenly, completely mislead a stranger, who cannot catch sight in their close
depths of any friendly landmark of steeple or tower to guide his

Fig. 2.—Birthplace of Rubens.

steps aright. The house, once found, is easily distinguished from
others near it, as well from its size as from the inscriptions upon
it. It is a noble mansion, situated at a slight angle of the street.
The carved door-frame was added in the year 1729; in a medallion
over its centre is a portrait of Rubens, and on a shield above are
the arms of Marie de Medici. In the year 1822, two inscribed

tablets were placed between the windows on each side the
doorway, to which attention was called by large gilt stars above
them. One narrates the fact of Rubens's birth in the mansion;
the other, the death, in the same house, of Marie de Medici, the
widow of Henry IV. of France, the mother of Louis XIII., and the
mother-in-law of three sovereigns, among them Henrietta Maria,
wife to our Charles I., who was by the intrigues of the Cardinal
Richelieu compelled to exile herself, living for many years an
unhappy fugitive in various countries,* and ultimately dying at
Cologne, where her heart was buried near the high altar, but
her body removed to France. The glory of the house, as the
birthplace of Rubens, is somewhat saddened by the melancholy
end of this once-powerful royal patroness of the painter. She is
said to have died in the same chamber where he was born.†

In the Church of St. Peter, a few hundred yards from the house
of his birth, the infant Rubens was christened. It still preserves
a certain picturesque quaintness, which belongs to the past, and
does not disturb the mind of one who might dream he saw the
christening procession of the baby-boy destined to be so great a
painter and so distinguished a man hereafter.‡ John Rubens had

---

* She lived for some time in England, but was compelled to leave it in 1641, when
Lilly, the famous astrologer, who saw her, describes her as an "aged, lean, decrepit, poor
queen, ready for her grave; necessitated to depart hence, having no place of residence in
this world but where the courtesy of her hard fortune assigned it."

† The inscription on the house informs us that "he was the seventh child of his parents,
who resided here twenty years;" that his father died here, and was buried in the Church of
St. Peter.

‡ One of the last acts of Rubens's life was done in affectionate memory of the church of
his baptism. He painted for it an altar-piece, representing the Crucifixion of St. Peter, the

already a son born to him in this good city in the year 1574, but his second son was born three years afterwards, that is, on the 29th of June, 1577. That day being the festival of SS. Peter and Paul, the infant was carried to the Church of St. Peter, and christened Peter Paul Rubens, a name never to be forgotten in art. Let us enter the cloister, and walk beneath its arches toward the narrow door of the sacred building. Poverty is not without its picturesque features, in the beggars that lean against the wall, or sink upon their knees beside the gate, awaiting the approach of worshippers, whose charity they then solicit. The group inside the building has an equally marked individuality; the rich bourgeois and his family can be readily distinguished from the prosperous farmer, the peasantry are unlike both, as they are unlike each other, for the dwellers on this side the Rhine are very different from those on the other side of the noble river. Society has not here assumed the dead level of English uniformity. There is a local pride in local habits which no great modern scheme of centralization has yet destroyed. We see little in the scene before us that might not have met the eye on the day when the unconscious baby of the Rubens family was formally admitted a

---

patron saint of the edifice. It depicts the martyrdom, with the saint's head downward, and is more remarkable for the striking character of the scene than for general merit. Rubens thought highly of it, and in one of his letters to his friend Gildorp talks of it as one of his best works. But Sir Joshua Reynolds says, " Many parts of this picture are so feebly drawn, and with so tame a pencil, that I cannot help suspecting that Rubens died before he had completed it, and that it was finished by some of his scholars." The picture was taken by the French to Paris, but has since been restored to its original place over the altar; the copy made to supply the place when it was absent is that constantly exhibited,—the original is at its back.

member of the Roman Catholic Church. At one corner of the
building still stands the remarkable font in which he was
christened. It is of bronze, shaped like a large chalice, and bears
date "Anno 1569" upon the rim. The bowl is decorated with the
arms of the city—three royal crowns upon a fess—alluding to the

Fig. 3.— Font in St. Peter's Church, Cologne.

heads of the three Magi, once popularly termed "the three
Kings of Cologne," still preserved as a sacred relic in the Cathedral of Cologne, first brought there by the Emperor Frederick
Barbarossa in the twelfth century, and which wondrously enriched
the city in the middle ages by the number of pilgrims drawn

towards their shrine.* The summit of the cover is decorated with figures representing the baptism of the Saviour by St. John, attended with angels, the sacred dove descending on the apex.

At the early age of ten years Rubens lost the fostering care of a father. He had known no other home but Cologne, but his mother reverted to her earlier one in Antwerp. Fearful scenes of strife had been enacted in that city, as Protestant or Catholic faction gained the ascendancy; but now the Duke of Parma had subjugated its hostile inhabitants to the Emperor Maximilian II. and the Catholic faith. In 1588 the widowed mother of Rubens was again located with her family in Antwerp. Her position and connections enabled her to place him as a page, at the age of sixteen, with another widowed lady, the Countess of Lalaing. But the life was irksome to the lad,—irksome by the very indolence and irregularity that would be its great charm to an unintellectual boy. Rubens's father was a scholar and a gentleman, and he made his sons the same. When Peter Paul returned to his mother's house after a few months' servitude, she well understood the lad's reasons for so doing; for she was also no ordinary person, and her affectionate education and wise council were as lovingly

---

* This shrine is still one of the most remarkable upon the Continent. It consists of a case covered with plates of silver-gilt, enriched with chasing, and laid out in arcades, enclosing figures of saints and prophets, and highly embellished with jewels and antique sculptured stones. The skulls of the three kings repose within, and may be seen from an opening in the centre. They are crowned, and have their names formed in rubies on each. Many of the jewels which once enriched this shrine were removed, to support those monks who carried it to Westphalia for safety, at the time when the French Republicans were masters of the city of Cologne.

acknowledged by her son in after life as any mother could wish ; for when, prosperous and happy in the palaces of Genoa, the painter was in full enjoyment of fame, profit, and pleasure, he broke away from all, to hurry post-haste to her sick-room.   Alas! she died before he reached it, and the disconsolate young artist shut himself up for four months in the Abbey of St. Michael, where she lay buried, mourning thus long a loss that was irreparable to him.

Thanks to the innate goodness of woman—uncorrupted by that closer business connection with the world which sometimes hardens man's heart—there are few among us that cannot testify to the loving care of a mother's guidance. There is nothing so precious while it remains with us ; there is no loss so great as that loss.   Rubens always felt it was to his mother's judgment, prudence, and care that he owed the due appreciation of his intellectual struggles. Freed from the servile duties of a page, he was placed to study law, that he might follow his father's profession ; but, as he showed much love for drawing, his tendency was indulged by permission to relax his mind in the art he loved. That love became a passion, and he earnestly petitioned that his future profession might be that of a painter.   On due consideration, it was allowed him ; but he was unfortunate in the selection of his first master, the landscape painter Verhaegt, with whom he had little sympathy ; and still less with his second one, Van Oort, the historical painter, a man of dissolute life and coarse manners, repulsive to a gentle and gentlemanly mind, like that of Rubens. His third master was in every way fitted for him—a well-educated man, with elegant tastes, and kindly and refined manners.   Otho

Venius* became the tutor and friend of the great scholar committed to his charge. This artist was court-painter to the Archduke Albert, the governor of the Netherlands, and he has received the honourable appellation of "the Flemish Raphael," and not without reason, as his graceful pictures will show, many of which are the treasured decorations of the Antwerp churches to this day. In that of St. Andrew are several; the best being "St. Matthew called by the Saviour from the Receipt of Customs," it has more of Raphael's simplicity of design, purity of colour, and unobtrusive beauty than we see in any of his followers. He was a very perfect draughtsman, and designed a large number of book illustrations.† To all his early masters, therefore, we may trace some of the peculiarities of Rubens's manner, though his genius surpassed them all and was trammelled by none. His power of landscape painting, which—unlike historic painters—he occasionally practised for itself, and not for his backgrounds merely, he may have imbibed from Verhaegt; his love of bold and vigorous colour in figure-painting from Van Oort, who was chiefly remarkable for that quality; and his fondness for graceful infantine forms from Venius. We copy from the "Emblems of Love,"‡ by that artist,

---

* His proper Flemish name, Otho Van Veen, he had thus Latinized, in conformity with a custom popular at that time in the Low Countries, and which induced Gerritz of Rotterdam to alter his into that of Erasmus, by which only he is now known.

† His principal works are the "Roman Wars," engraved by Tempesta; the "Historia Septem Infantum de Lara," with forty spirited engravings by the same artist; a folio of emblematic pictures of Human Life; and a small oblong quarto volume of Emblems of Love, the most graceful and beautiful of all which he designed.

‡ The original title of the work ran thus, "Amorum Emblemata, figuris æneis incisa

two figures. One, which he calls "Love untrammelled," has just
spurned a bridle on the ground, and is flying upward joyfully : the
other, termed "Contented Thoughts," shows Cupid in a well-
cushioned chair, contemplating his fair one's picture with secret

Fig. 4.—" Love untrammelled," after
Otho Venius.

Fig. 5.—" Contented Thoughts," after
Otho Venius.

satisfaction. Both call to mind similar figures by Rubens,
who delighted in such quaint imaginings, offsprings of poetic
thought.

Happy in the house of a noble-minded and accomplished
man, the scholar-days of Rubens passed cheerfully onward. No
painter possessed greater industry than he, none laboured more
unceasingly at the technics of art; he fortunately had a friend
and a master in Venius, who, less great than his pupil ultimately

studio Othonis Væni. Antwerpum venalia apud auctorem M.D.C.IIX" (1608). Prefixed
are recommendatory Latin verses by Daniel Heinsius and Philip Rubens, the painter's elder
brother. These cuts were afterwards used to illustrate Quarles's " Emblems," London.

became, was naturally of more refined mind, and had a purer and less sensuous love of beauty. It is impossible to over-estimate the utility of judicious control and criticism such as he would give to a young man like Rubens, whose natural vigour and bold conception wanted just such wholesome correction as Venius could impart. The refinement of manners, the courtier-like air, and the cultivated tastes of the master, were all fully appreciated by the scholar : and his example, no doubt, confirmed Rubens's own love for collecting and studying the best works, ancient and modern. There is no better instance of a man who more generally profited by the experiences of life in its upward and onward course than Rubens presents. He may be said to have spent his days in constant self-improvement, so that he became not only a great painter, but a learned man ; not only an artist of world-wide renown, but an ambassador from his own sovereign to other kings, and their companion and friend. Surely no man ever upheld the artistic character more nobly than he.

Venius having fully instructed Rubens in the arcana of his profession, and seeing he was as well grounded in general knowledge, advised him to visit Italy. The advice was taken, and, in the middle of the year 1600, he started on his journey, well provided with due introductions from the Archduke Albert, who already esteemed him. His journey lay through Venice to Mantua, where he presented himself to the Duke Vincenzio Gonzaga, who received him most favourably ; and, on better acquaintance, offered to attach him to his service as gentleman of his chamber ; a position Rubens readily accepted, as it allowed him full liberty of studying the ducal collection, then celebrated as one of the finest in Italy. It was this that gave the painter his peculiar knowledge of antique art, more particularly as exhibited on medals, coins, and intaglios, minor works as regards size, but often as great in treatment as colossal marbles. It was this that led him in after life to collect such objects for himself, and it was this that gave him his great facility in designing an abundance of works now comparatively little known, such as book illustrations, designs for pageantry, triumphal arches, &c., which he was often called on to execute; and all of them show how his fertile fancy was grounded on the best works of the ancient artists, though he never allowed them to cripple his own native genius. His classic tastes led him to reflect with pleasure on such works as depicted scenes from their history; but his native bias led him to delight chiefly in the gorgeous richness of their ceremonial observances. Hence Andrea Mantegna's "Triumphs of Cæsar"* riveted his attention most; there was a wealth of display in this scenic work which accorded with the young Fleming's mind, and he copied one of the compartments, not, however, without some vigorous variation, the creation of his own warmer imagination. With permission of the duke he visited Rome, but necessarily stayed there but for a limited time; he afterwards visited Venice, and his experience of the greatness of their colourists had a strongly

---

* These pictures passed into the collection of our King Charles I., and are still upon the walls of the palace at Hampton. Outlines from them were engraved by Andrea Andreani on wood, somewhere about the year 1600, and in 1858 Mr. Henry Duke lithographed nine of them. They rank only second to the celebrated cartoons of Raffaelle.

marked effect on his after works. On his return to Mantua, the
duke gave him the greatest proofs of his esteem and confidence; he had in Rubens a gentlemanly companion as well as a
highly-informed artist; and he selected him as the most fitting
person to convey to the king, Philip the Third of Spain, a present
of a state carriage and horses he had obtained for that purpose.
The artist accepted the charge; and became as popular at the court
of Madrid as he was at that of the Duke of Mantua. He painted
while there several portraits of the king and the nobles, and
returned loaded with presents and compliments to the duke, whom
he left soon afterward, to return to Rome, and finish the commission he had given him to copy the works of the greatest masters
there. Rubens's elder brother Philip accompanied him to "the
eternal city," and studied its antiquities with him. Their conjoined
labours appeared in a volume; the literary part being by the
more learned Philip, but in which Peter Paul had a share, and he
executed the designs which embellish it. We have before noted
Rubens's connection with the press, which continued all his life;
and when he left Rome and got back to Genoa, he busily sketched
the ancient buildings of the noble old city; on his return to
Antwerp they were published in a folio volume.*

This return to Antwerp was expedited by the melancholy news
of his mother's last illness. How it affected him we have already
noted; on his slow recovery from the mental blow, he thought of

---

* It comprises 139 views, and was published in 1622. A second series was published
thirty years afterwards.

again going to Mantua. He visited Brussels, to take leave of his patrons, the Archduke Ferdinand and his wife the Infanta Isabella; they received him most graciously, and gladly welcomed him to his country; and he ultimately decided on staying there; but, anxious that the pompous nothings of a courtier's life should not distract him from his art, he decided on making the quiet old city of Antwerp his home; and that it might be a home in its most perfect sense, he married the daughter of one of its magistrates, Elizabeth Brant, and built himself a house in the city of his adoption.

His marriage took place in November, 1609; the building of his house was not so quickly effected. The love of Italy and its home-life induced a desire on his part to construct his new home more in the Italian than the Flemish taste. He obtained a piece of ground of the guild of Arquebusiers, who then possessed it,* and upon it erected, from his own designs, a palatial house, such as fell to the lot of few artists to obtain. It still exists, but it is much shorn of its exuberant ornament; this, which was its great fault, was still characteristic of the mind of its master. He had a

---

* The arrangement he made with them was, that he should, in return for the land, paint a picture for them representing their patron, St. Christopher. Rubens seems to have felt their arrangement as a liberal one, and was anxious to carry it out as liberally on his own part. He gave them in return the far-famed work, now the glory of Antwerp Cathedral, "The Descent from the Cross," considered as his master-piece. This great picture is the centre of a large triptich, or double-winged altar-piece, the wings acting as shutters to close over the picture. The back and front of each wing is painted in other subjects, the outer ones exhibiting the story of St. Christopher, which would always be seen when the whole was closed. The painter thus gave them five pictures instead of the promised one.

taste for the fanciful combination of forms which produce the
sensation of splendour, and in his works he constantly shows
a tendency to obtain this, even at the sacrifice of consistency. It
was so in his house : and though its details were founded on the

Fig. 6.—Courtyard of Rubens's Mansion.

classic style of the ancients, it was overloaded with the debase-
ments of the Italian Revivalists, upon which Rubens added his
own fanciful displays, which no architect would probably countenance. He succeeded, however, in defiance of rule, in "com-
posing" a very stately and highly-decorated mansion. It stands

D

in a narrow street leading from the principal thoroughfare, the
Place de Mer, nearly opposite the Exchange, and in the best part
of the city. The courtyard was connected with a large garden
by a triumphal arch; on the right was the mansion, on the left

Fig. 7.—Rubens's Summer-house.

the offices. We engrave this part of the building, as it affords the
best idea of Rubens's general taste in sumptuous design.

The garden of Rubens's house, though confined, as all town-
gardens must be, was nevertheless large for its situation, and
comprised green alleys, pleasant parterres, and a summer-house

he has immortalised in many pictures. The situation of this structure may be noted in our view of the courtyard. Harrewyns published views, in 1692, of the house and grounds, and from that
print we copy our representation of this summer-house, where
Rubens and his friends passed many happy hours. Like all

Fig. 8.—Rubens's Château at Stein.

other architectural designs of the painter, it is extremely fanciful
—a style which may be termed "Rubenesque" pervades it; but
it is a style that met with much favour in the Low Countries,
and may be seen frequently repeated in Belgium and Holland.

Rubens also possessed the château at Stein, on the road

between Malines and Vilvorde, a country-house equally fitted for
the residence of a noble. It is a characteristic building, now fast
decaying, surrounded by a moat, which adds to its damp and
gloom ; but has been immortalized by its master, during its best
days, in several good pictures ; one of the best, embracing the
rich view over the fertile country obtained from its windows, now
graces our National Gallery. It must be owned that Rubens has
made the scene a little more poetic than it appears to an ordinary
eye, but he certainly studied for his charming landscapes in the
immediate vicinity of his own residence.

The great Fleming, now well established in his picturesque
home in the old city of Antwerp, gave scope to the tastes which
governed his mind. His house and its appurtenances had that
sumptuous and fanciful style which characterized his pictures ; *
its interior was further enriched by masterpieces of art, selected
with judgment wherever he could obtain them ; and in collecting
he was guided by the advice of the best men, who were constantly
aiding him to increase his store.

Rubens's home-life has thus been narrated by his biographers :
He rose very early, and made a point of commencing his day by
religious devotion. After breakfasting, he went to his painting-
room, and while at work received visitors, and talked with them
freely ; or, in their absence, listened to some one who read to him
from the pages of the finest writers, his love for the classics

---

* Houbraken tells us that upon the construction of this mansion Rubens spent 60,000
florins.

inducing him to give preference to the best Roman authors, he himself being a thoroughly good Latin scholar. At midday he took a frugal dinner; for he had taught himself to think that loading the stomach clogged the fancy. By this custom he was enabled to go to work again after his meal, and continue till the evening; and but for this rule he could never have executed one tithe of his commissions. At the close of the day he rode for several miles, and on his return passed the evening in agreeable converse with the friends who visited his house : they comprised the best society of the day, and in their company he would examine and descant on his fine collection of coins, prints, and antiques, or take steps to increase it by any means they could point out,—for Rubens was an ardent " collector" and a liberal purchaser, esteeming money, not for itself, but for the intellectual pleasures it procured him. Thus the artist of princely mind lived like a prince, except that his courtiers were not the self-seeking parasites of courts in general, but the friends who loved him for his own sake, and for the pleasure his society gave them, binding them by his countenance into one brotherhood.

The print published by Harrewyns, in 1684, exhibits the studio of Rubens, at that time converted into a bed-chamber, and which we here copy. It is lighted from the roof. The elder Disraeli thus speaks of it : * " This princely artist perhaps first contrived for his studio the apartment with a dome, like the rotunda of the

* " Curiosities of Literature," vol. iii.

Pantheon, where the light, descending from an aperture or window at top, sent down a single equal light—that perfection of light which distributes its magical effect on the objects beneath. This was his precious museum, where he had collected a vast number of books, which were intermixed with his marbles, statues, cameos, intaglios, and all that variety of the riches of art which

Fig. 9.—Room in Rubens's House.

he had drawn from Rome.* But the walls did not yield in value, for they were covered by pictures of his own composition, or copies by his own hand, made at Venice and Madrid, of Titian and

* In the appendix to Carpenter's " Pictorial Notices of Vandyke" is printed the correspondence between himself and Sir Dudley Carleton, offering to exchange some of his own pictures for antiques in possession of the latter, who was ambassador from England to Holland, and who collected also for the Earl of Arundel.

Paul Veronese. No foreigners, men of letters, lovers of the arts, or even princes, would pass through Antwerp without visiting the house of Rubens, to witness the animated residence of genius, and the great man who had conceived the idea. Yet great as was his mind, and splendid as were the habits of his life, he could not resist the entreaties of the 100,000 florins of our Duke of Buckingham to dispose of his studio. The great artist could not, however, abandon for ever the delightful contemplations he was depriving himself of, and as substitutes for the miracles of art he had lost, he solicited and obtained leave to replace them by casts, which were scrupulously deposited in the places where the originals had been." There can be no higher compliment paid from man to man than was paid by Sir Dudley Carleton, after the amicable exchange he made with Rubens of his own antiques for some of the artist's pictures :—" I cannot subscribe to your denial of being a prince, because I esteem you the prince of painters, and of gentlemen, and to that end I kiss your hands." Such language from an ambassador to an artist, on the conclusion of a bargain, sheds honour on both.

Rubens always felt the true dignity of his own character ; he never forfeited it by any unworthy act, nor would he ever allow it to be lowered by any false estimate from any source. When John, Duke of Braganza, afterwards King of Portugal, desired him, during his stay at Madrid, to pay him a visit, at his famed hunting-seat, the Villa Viciosa, the artist accepted the invitation, and set out with so large a number of servants, that the noble duke took fright at the expense so large a retinue might impose

—

on him ; and despatched a messenger to meet Rubens half-way, with an apology of "sudden and unavoidable absence," on the part of the duke, and an offer of a purse of fifty pistoles to indemnify the artist for the expenses of his journey. Rubens met the meanness with a dignity that reversed the position of the artist and the prince. "Give the duke my most dutiful regards," said he, "and assure him of my great regret at not personally paying those respects his invitation led me to hope to do. It was to assure his highness of my best services that I set out, and so far was I from expecting fifty pistoles toward paying my expenses, that I have already with me one thousand such pieces, which will more than serve my need."

It was this princely mind, and clear honesty of conduct, combined with the style of an educated gentleman, that made Rubens the companion of princes, and ultimately an ambassador of state. He had met our Duke of Buckingham in Paris, in April, 1625, and afterwards at Antwerp, in the September of the same year ; and the intimacy led to the employ of Rubens in state affairs, by the Infanta Isabella, who had often found his advice useful, and felt that the painter could negotiate best in her affairs, and endanger their issue less than any other person, as his ostensible mission was art, not politics. He conducted his business with remarkable tact. In our own State Paper Office his letters are still preserved, and, in 1858, they were edited by Mr. Sainsbury. They possess a high and noble tone, dignity, firmness, and cautiousness, exquisitely united to the most polite courtesy, elegant composition, and elevated sentiment, and at once show the education of the gentleman, and the mind of the man. In 1628 the Earl of Carlisle met Rubens in the house of Vandyke, at Antwerp, and he has written a very graphic account of the interview to the Duke of Buckingham, which gives a good idea of the painter's earnest diplomacy in aid of a peace between England and Spain. The Abbé de Scaglia writes to the Earl of Carlisle: —"The King of Spain, the more to qualify the Sieur Rubens, and to give the greater reputation to his negotiation, has declared him secretary of his privy council, a reason why his Majesty should esteem him the more and yourself also." All this led to a journey to Spain, after the assassination, in the same year, of the Duke of Buckingham,—that country's implacable enemy,—and the ultimate happy settlement of a peace. Rubens, on his return, immediately started for England, which he reached in May, 1629, in a ship expressly sent to Dunkirk, by King Charles I., for his use. In England he was most honourably received, lodged in the house of Sir Balthazar Gerbier, and all his expenses paid by Charles, who knighted him on the 21st of February, 1630, allowing him to add to his coat of arms a canton containing the lion of England : the University of Cambridge also conferred on him the honorary degree of master of arts.

His political career ceased with the life of the Infanta Isabella in 1633, and he henceforward gave his undivided attention to art, although Charles had offered him a pension if he would remove to Brussels, and act there as political agent to the English Government—an offer he at once refused, as it would depose, or interfere with, his respected friend Gerbier. Of his industry in his art we

E

have already spoken; but it took a more discursive range than among most artists. He did not paint only, but furnished an abundance of designs for varied purposes. One of Gerbier's letters tells of "certain drawings of the said Sir P. Rubens for carving of cups," intended for the use of the celebrated collector of art and *vertu*, Thomas Howard, Earl of Arundel. He also furnished numerous designs for books; and the productions of the world-renowned press of Plantyn, of Antwerp, were frequently decorated with emblematic title-pages, full of originality and power. Like Raphael, he employed the best engravers to copy his works under his own superintendence; and he drew upon wood many good designs, fully aware of the large renown that Albert Dürer had achieved by the same process.* We also find him working on missals, and never avoiding anything that could promote the general love of art among all classes of society. Of his architectural tastes we have already spoken. He furnished the design for the façade of the Church of S. Carlo Borromeo, at Antwerp, one of the most striking relics of the past grandeur of the old city preserved for our time: it was constructed by the

---

* These woodcuts are generally much larger than Dürer's, but do not possess that cleanness of line and knowledge of pen-drawing which Dürer's evince. They have more solid shadow, and their painter-like style has been sometimes aided by tint-blocks printed over them, after the manner of the Italian, Ugo da Carpi. The largest of his cuts is the somewhat offensive subject, Susannah and the Elders; it measures 22½ inches in breadth by 17 in height. The next in size, and the best in treatment, is a Repose of the Holy Family, remarkable for the freedom and beauty of the trees and landscape: it is a copy of one of his best known pictures. But perhaps the most characteristic is a group of Fauns supporting Silenus: it is admirably rendered. All were engraved by Christopher Jegher, whose chief ability lay in the preservation of Rubens's powerful *chiar'-oscuro*.

Jesuits, and enriched with costly marbles, taken by the Spaniards from an Algerine corsair,—which was conveying them to Constantinople for the erection of a mosque,—brought to Cadiz, and sold

Fig. 10.—Church of S. Carlo Borromeo.

to an Antwerp merchant. Rubens enriched this structure with many fine paintings; of these, thirty-nine upon the vaulting, the subjects taken from sacred history, afford extraordinary proof of

his talent at foreshortening. They were fortunately copied by De
Witt, and afterwards engraved by Jean Punt, and published at
Amsterdam in 1751, for the church was almost destroyed by fire,
occasioned by lightning, in the year 1718—the façade in part, and
the chapel of the Virgin adjoining, are all that remain as Rubens
designed them. The latter is exceedingly picturesque in its
arrangement, covered with paintings, decorated with statuary, and
enriched with costly marbles.* Though the architect may justly
consider the works of Rubens meretricious, they hit the popular
taste of the day; and his love of display, and fondness for
mythological embodiment, led to his employ by the town-council
of Antwerp, when Ferdinand and Isabella made their triumphal
entry into that city in 1642, to design the triumphal arches, and
other pageants with which the senate of Antwerp greeted its
imperial rulers; and they all exhibit, in a striking manner, the
painter's love for scenic effects. Unlike Raffaelle, who studied
the frescoes of the baths of Titus, and founded on them a style of
ornament refined by his own gentle graces, the Antwerp artist
saw only as much in the grand remains of ancient architecture as
would allow him to indulge in a bold and bizarre combination of
its most striking features with his own powerful imaginings.†

---

* This church was used as an hospital for the wounded English soldiers after the Battle
of Waterloo.

† His friend Gevartius published a noble folio volume descriptive of the great doings on
this occasion, with admirably executed plates by Sandrart and Bolswert, under Rubens's
superintendence. In the public picture gallery of Antwerp are still preserved the original
designs for some of these gorgeous pageants, boldly painted by the hand of Rubens himself.

Though now we test these works by a purer standard of taste, there is little doubt that it was necessary, in the first instance, to popularise the style, and prune it of redundancies afterwards. Rubens aided the general movement, and, by gaining attention to the picturesque, paved the way for a chaster study of ancient architecture.

In all these labours he was aided by many assistants, and his school embraced the best men of his age and country, who, after his death, nobly upheld Flemish art. Rubens never disowned their assistance, or concealed its true character. Thus, in the list of pictures sent to Carleton, he notes, "Prometheus bound on Mount Caucasus, with an eagle which pecks his liver. Original, by my hand, and the eagle done by Snyders.—Leopards, taken from life, with satyrs and nymphs. Original, by my hand, except a most beautiful landscape, by the hand of a master skilful in that department." When not is own, he notes, "by one of my scholars, the whole, however, retouched by my hand." His pictures have been trebly classified by Dr. Waagen, as—painted by himself; by his pupils after his sketches, and retouched by him; or copies of well-known pictures by him, similarly corrected. Vandyke and Jordaens were his greatest assistants: the former stood alone after Rubens's death, and the latter enjoyed the reputation of being the greatest successor in the master's peculiar style: Snyders took his independent course as a vigorous painter of hunting-scenes; and his other pupil, David Teniers, the elder, struck out a new path—the delineation of the manners of the peasants of the Low Countries. They again had their followers; and thus the genius of Rubens, like a fruitful tree, branched forth and blossomed over the land, when its root laid low in the ground.

In the picture gallery of Antwerp is still preserved the chair in which the painter usually sat. It is mounted on a pedestal

Fig. 11.—Rubens's Chair.

within a glass case, and appears to have been subjected to daily wear, with all that constancy with which an artist uses a piece of furniture to which he is habituated: the leathern seat has been broken through in many places, and has been carefully drawn together by strong threads. The leathern back is ornamented with gilding stamped upon it, and in the centre are the arms of Rubens, above which appears his name, thus:—" Pet. Paul. Rubens : " below is the date 1623.

Rubens was twice married :* his second wife was a beautiful girl of sixteen, his niece, Helena Forman, whose features are well known by their endless multiplication in his works; for he was not only fond of painting her portrait, but adopting her features for the beauties of his fancy subjects. The painter, at the period of his second marriage, had reached the somewhat advanced age of fifty-four, but he had manners which concealed his years, and in the paintings where he is represented with his young wife we are never struck by the discrepancy of their ages. Rubens had a somewhat *soldatesque* style, and his wife had a comeliness beyond her years : the picture at Blenheim, in which she is depicted in all the glory of her beauty, attended by a page, sufficiently attests this ; as another picture in the same collection, and which was presented by the city of Brussels to the great Duke of Marlborough, tells of the painter's happy home. The scene is the garden of his house at Antwerp : Rubens is proudly and lovingly walking beside his wife, who conducts their child in leading strings. The painter wisely made his home his world; he gathered there, with no niggard hand, all that could make life pleasant, and few passed life so happily.

---

* His first wife died in the summer of 1626. He remained a widower until December, 1630, when he again married. His political travels occupied much of his time while single, and calmed his mind by a change of scene. It was during this time that he visited France Spain, and England.

There is a good anecdote told of him, which well illustrates the felicitous common sense of the man. An English student of alchemy made the painter magnificent promises of fortune by aid of the science if he would furnish the necessary funds for his laboratory. Princes were found at this time to entertain seriously hopes of thus enriching themselves. The painter merely replied, "You are here too late, by full twenty years ; for since that time I have found the art of making gold by aid of this palette and pencils."

In 1640 Rubens died. A letter from his old friend, Sir B. Gerbier, dated Brussels, May 21, 1640, notes, " Sir Peter Rubens is deadly sick ; the physicians of this toune being sent unto him for to try their best skill on him." In another letter, written to King Charles I. on the same day, he adds a postscript—" Since I finished this letter news is come of Sir Peter Rubens's death." He had died on the 20th of May, 1640,* aged sixty years, " of a deflaction which fell on his heart, after some days of indisposition and gout. He is much regretted and commended : hath left a rich widow and rich children." He was buried on May 23, in the vault belonging to his wife's family, in the Church of St. James, at

---

* Mr. Sainsbury, in a note to his book, adds—" It has always been said that Rubens died on May 30, 1640 ; but the ten days' difference between the old and the new style, from the year 1582 to 1699, must always be taken into account when fixing the date of an event which occurs in a Roman Catholic country. The Gregorian, or reformed calendar, was not used in England until September, 1752. An act was then passed, ordering the day following, the 2nd of September, to be reckoned the 14th, which allowed eleven days for the discrepancies of the old and new styles during the eighteenth century."

Antwerp. His funeral was conducted with much pomp, attended by the chief personages in Antwerp, the officers of the city, and the members of the Academy of Painting. Sixty boys of the Orphan Asylum walked beside the bier, each carrying a lighted taper. The church was hung throughout with black velvet, the

Fig. 12.—Rubens's Chapel.

service being performed in the sumptuous manner usually adopted for the nobility. His widow afterwards endowed the chapel given in our view, and erected in it the altar there represented. The picture above the altar-table is from the painter's own hand. It represents the Virgin with the Infant Saviour in her lap, surrounded by saints, among whom stands St. George in full armour,

F

which is a portrait of Rubens, the female saints beside him being portraits of his wives, and St. Jerome that of his father. It is a family group as well as a sacred picture. Above it is a marble statue of the Virgin, which is attributed to Du Quesnoy, better

Fig. 13.—Rubens's Monument.

known as Fiamingo. The small crucifix standing upon the altar-table is said to be that which was used by Rubens himself in his private devotions. The central slab in front of the altar covers the grave of the master: it has a very long inscription from the pen of the learned Gevartius, the intimate friend of the painter,

celebrating his ability as a painter, and his knowledge as a man
" of all the arts and elegancies of every age," and that he
" happily laid the foundation of the peace " between England and
Spain.   Beneath are a few lines to record the restoration of this
monument in 1755 by Jacques de Parys, a canon of this church,
" a descendant of Rubens through his mother and grandmother—
descendants of Rubens in the male line having become extinct."

An inventory of the pictures in his house at his death was
sent by Gerbier to Charles I.   The late Dawson Turner published a limited number of copies for private distribution, and
Mr. Sainsbury recently reprinted it in his " Life of Rubens from
Unpublished Papers," in 1858.   The number and value of these
works of art are strikingly illustrative of the character and
position of the man : they equally show his attachment to his
profession, and the extent of his pecuniary resources.   They are
said to have produced the sum of £25,000.   It was the intention of
the family to have sold them by auction, but they were sold
separately by private contract, having been valued by Snyders,
Wildens, and Moermans.   The King of Spain secured the gems,
medals, and carvings, as well as some of the best pictures ; the
Emperor of Germany, the King of Poland, the Elector of Bavaria,
and Cardinal Richelieu, were the next most important purchasers.
The collection was particularly rich in pictures by Titian, Paul
Veronese, and Tintoretto, and a very many copies—" made in
Spaine, Italie, and other places, as well after Titian as other good
masters."   There were ninety-four pictures by his own hand,
among them that which his widow presented to adorn the chapel

of the tomb of her husband—the famous *Chapeau de Paille* ;* many
landscapes, portraits, and other subjects, probably kept as studies
by the painter, or from some interesting association—for he had
more demands for his work than he could satisfy. His collection
of pictures by the old masters comprise specimens by John Van
Eyck, Albert Dürer, Lucas Van Leyden, Holbein, Quintyn Matsys,
&c., proving the catholicity of his tastes. Of the masters of his
own era, he had works by Vandyke,† Snyders, Jordaens, De
Vos, Breughel, &c. In short, it was the gallery of a noble of
refined taste.

The solemn old city of Antwerp feels still honourable pride in
its great painter, of whom it has been well said, " there was the
same breadth and magnificence in his character as in the colour of
his compositions, and his mind was as free from littleness as his
works." In 1840, at the great fête in honour of Rubens, his
statue, of colossal proportions, by Geefs, was uncovered. It stands
in the centre of the *Place Verte*, the great public square

---

* Described in the catalogue as " The picture of a woman with her hands one upon
another." Rubens would never part with this picture, which he had painted from a
Mademoiselle Lundens, to whose family it passed after the death of his widow, and
remained with their descendants until the year 1822, when it was purchased by M. Niewen-
huys for 36,000 florins, and brought to England. After being offered in vain to George IV.,
it was bought by the late Sir Robert Peel for 3,500 guineas.

† Among them was the " Betrayal of Christ," which the painter had presented to
Rubens as a love-gift before he went to Italy. It is still in Antwerp. Rubens had found
young Vandyke poor ; he had made him rich by purchasing his unsold pictures, taking him
into his own studio, and ultimately enabling him to start for study in Italy, giving him a
horse for the journey. Rubens hung his parting gift in the best position in his house, and
took constant pleasure in pointing out its merits to his visitors.

immediately beside the old cathedral, whose picturesque towers form an admirable background to the scene. England may learn a useful lesson here, and not practically deny her own intellectually great sons, by refusing them that public recognition which she so willingly accords to statesmen and warriors. While they are often forgotten or uncared for by another generation,

" The artist never dies."

His works reflect greatness and glory on his country for ever; his victory is one of peace and goodwill, appealing to, and conquering by, the best feelings of our nature; and when presented to our view in the manly type of Rubens, commands honour and esteem from all.

RUBENS AND VANDYKE:—ART-RAMBLES IN BELGIUM.

VANDYKE'S HOUSE.

RUBENS AND VANDYKE:—ART-RAMBLES IN BELGIUM.

CHAPTER I.

OPPOSITE our own coasts, and separated from them by a short sea-passage, the kingdom of Belgium possesses claims on the attention of the lovers of art and history superior to any other near neighbour. The early history of England is much mixed up with that of the Low Countries; and to the Englishman, whose love of liberty is at once honest and

profound, the actions of the brave men who so perseveringly fought
against spiritual and regal tyranny when the hope of victory was
indeed a forlorn one, must ever be dear. In the marshes of
Holland and Belgium liberty made her last grand stand,
emerging victorious, and giving to surrounding nations much
of her benign influence. The first great blow at feudalism was
struck by the brave Flemish burghers; and the basis upon
which modern commerce rests had its foundations laid by them
also.

The wealthy burghers were not mere tradesmen; they loved
art and literature, and patronised both in a most catholic spirit.
The taste permeated all ranks; thus the trade-guilds, or fraternities of workmen, instituted their "Chambers of Rhetoric,"
and concocted dramatic moralisations, often thought worthy to
amuse kings and nobles, when *joyeuse entrées* gave these honest
workers a chance of testifying their loyalty and respect.

Nowhere can a greater or more sudden change be felt than
in the short passage between London and Antwerp. The most
disagreeable part of the voyage takes place in the night, when
the steamboat becomes a floating hotel. The morning is passed
in the windings of the Scheldt; mid-day lands us at Antwerp,
amid scenes that recall the memories of three hundred years.
The past mingles with the present so quaintly and so charmingly,
that the student of art and history may be envied his first visit to
Antwerp.

As the mouth of the Scheldt is entered, the town of Flushing
gives token of a contrast to our own shores. The river is like an

arm of the sea, the town a walled and embattled gathering of quaint old houses in a lonely plain of sand, a solitary home for an amphibious race of hardy fishermen. Terneuse, a small village, with a finely painted church, a high-pitched roof and spire,

Fig. 15.—Warden.

and an abundance of weathercocks, is the next place passed ; then comes Warden (Fig. 15), of which we give the characteristic features in our small sketch. Doule soon succeeds it, a droll, Dutch-looking little place, with very few houses, and its church (a

Fig. 16.—Fort Lillo.

little cathedral, as all the Belgic churches appear to be), with a miniature steeple and spire, transepts, and west porch. Almost immediately afterwards we come in sight of Fort Lillo (Fig. 16), which, with its opposite brother, protects this part of the stream, and guards the approach to Antwerp. Nothing can afford a greater contrast than this river and the Thames; the one crowded with vessels, the other dull and lonely, yet fortified so strongly, while our own river, crowded with shipping, and lined with buildings, has a comparatively unprotected look. The Scheldt is a difficult river to navigate, but it once received vessels from all parts of the world; its windings are most tortuous, and it is a very sudden curve that brings Antwerp (Fig. 17) in sight, its group of spires

Fig. 17.— First View of Antwerp from the River.

and towers cutting against the sky in picturesque relief, and holding out fair promise of a pleasant sojourn to the traveller.

The *Place Verte*, on the south side of the cathedral, is the focus of life and gaiety. The tree-shadowed old square is the favourite resort of the idler, and will have strong attraction to the stranger, for it is one of the most picturesque localities in the old city. The entire length of the cathedral forms one of its boundaries; the quaint roof and spires of this building are nowhere seen to greater advantage. In the centre of the place stands Geefs's noble colossal statue of Rubens; and the Englishman may feel, in looking upon it, that he is in a country where men, mentally great, who devote themselves to the elevation of the higher emotions of life, are honoured and recognised. Rubens is "the bright particular star" of Antwerp; its inhabitants never tire of honouring his memory; his residence is still shown, his favourite chair is preserved in the Museum, every trifle in the town connected with him is held sacred. The people are, however, equally attached to the renown of other names that have made their city famous. Quintin Matsys and his history is familiar to every one; so is that of Vandyke. It is not too much to say that, while many great statesmen and warriors are forgotten, the artists of Belgium are familiarly and affectionately remembered by their country.

The frightful devastations produced by civil and religious wars in the sixteenth and seventeenth centuries, have robbed the churches of the vast accumulation of early art-treasures they possessed up to the time of Philip II. of Spain. The cruelty and intolerance of the court of Spain is without a parallel in European history, and after many years of sufferance was at last met by an ebullition that spared no relic of its dominance. We must, therefore, not look in the churches of Antwerp for antiquities, such mediæval relics as ecclesiologists of the present day delight to descant upon, nor for pictures that were painted by *real* "Pre-Raffaellites." We must be content to miss those that preceded the seventeenth century, particularly when we find such glorious works of that period as reward the seeker in every corner of the old city. Nowhere can Rubens be seen to such advantage; in fact, he can fully be comprehended only in the city of his residence; works displaying all his peculiarities of style and character throughout his long, industrious, and honourable life, are here. The "prince of artists" is still a ruler in Antwerp, and it would be difficult to find another city where an artist is so entirely honoured.

It is not requisite, nor do we propose to descant upon his works here, or narrate their number and titles; that has been long since fully and efficiently done elsewhere. In taking a rapid survey of Belgium and its art-works, we may merely point out noticeable pictures, elucidating them by sketches from, or rather dissections of, each picture. Architecture must come in for the due share of notice demanded by that important art, particularly as regards the quaint peculiarities that catch the eye of a stranger. All this, and other features of ordinary life in Belgium, must be embodied in our passing glance.

The war between the Papists and the Reformers was fought as desperately here as anywhere, with the alternations that "the chances of war" bring. Now the religion of Rome seems firmly fixed, and nowhere are the stately services of that faith more strikingly conducted than in Belgium. In Rome they partake too much of the festive, or theatric, in their style, and are wanting in the grandeur and dignity that give them so impressive a character here. The architecture and fittings of the churches are more in accordance with the solemn pomp of religion; "the glory of regality" seems to invest the national faith; and the gorgeous processions on great festivals, to which all knees bow, show the deep-seated reverence of the people.

The stranger will notice at many street-corners pleasing little groups of the Virgin and Child, before whom lamps are occasionally lighted. Some of these are of considerable antiquity; many

Fig. 18.

possess much native grace. We give two specimens of these canopied figures; in one instance (Fig. 18) the simplicity of nature alone has been aimed at; there is a *motive*, however, in the action

of the infant Saviour unusual in works of its class : He starts forth
from the embrace of the Holy Virgin, holding forth the cross of
redemption in the left hand, while the right welcomes the

Fig. 19.—The Madonna Triumphant.

humblest aspirant of the faith.   More of quaint, mediæval feeling
is exhibited in our second specimen (Fig 19).   Here the Virgin is
crowned and enthroned as Queen; her canopy is surmounted by
a flag; a circle of stars adds lustre to her crown; she bears a

sceptre in her right hand, and is really "the Queen of Heaven," as with the Roman faith, rather than the simple "Mother of Jesus," as the Protestants consider her. The Saviour here is a passive figure, playing a very secondary part, as is too often the case in the Church of Rome. That she is "the woman" of the Apocalypse is typified by the serpent beneath her feet; her divine triumph is shown by the cherubim about her.

It is not always that the Virgin is thus shown triumphant. Her woes are often made the visible stimulus for the devotion of the faithful. "Notre Dame de Sept Douleurs," is occasionally seen with seven poniards in her breast, typical of her spiritual wounds; occasionally with one only, as in the engraving (Fig. 20) of a statuette in the Church of St. Andrew, attached to one of the pillars of the nave.

Fig. 20.—"Notre Dame des Douleurs."

It is impossible to deny the great devotion of the lower classes to all church ceremonials. The poor repose on the faith and in the hope of a better world, to compensate the misery to them of the present one; hence the high altars of the churches are never without devout plebeian worshippers; and their quaint costumes and simple devotion have abundant elements of the picturesque (Figs. 21 and 22). The flat lands of Belgium and

Holland necessitate a peculiar head-dress for its peasantry. The strong winds that blow across these plains from the North Sea, would make any "broad-brimmed" head-covering perfectly unmanageable; so a strange bonnet has been invented, that is perched at an angle above the crown, with the narrowest brim possible, acting as "a sun-shade" for the eyes. The girls manage

Fig. 21.—Group at the Altar, Antwerp Cathedral.

to make up for the meagreness of the bonnet by the amplitude of the cap, and indulge in lappets of lace, as costly as they can afford (Figs. 23 and 24). In fine weather the bonnet is dispensed with, and then the cap shines forth in all its glory. The ladies of the middle class wear dark veils, like the Spanish mantilla: this custom may be traced to the days of Charles V. and the Spanish rule in the Netherlands.

Typical figures of Faith, more or less graceful, abound in the churches. In that of S. Carlo Borromeo—the sumptuous fane of the Jesuits—is a very elegant figure, borne on clouds, supporting the cross, and elevating the cup of the Eucharist (Fig. 25). The Church, under less triumphant influences, is seen in our second example (Fig. 26).

Fig. 22.—Priestly Costume.

No one can examine the Belgic churches without being forcibly struck by the abundance and superiority of the wood-carving with which they are enriched. With the utmost elaboration of hand-labour is combined a high artistic feeling, and a painter-like freedom of execution that gives these works a very high character. It may be a question whether there be fitness

Fig. 23.—Head-dresses of Flemish Peasantry.

in converting a pulpit into a group of figures and accessories embodying a scriptural story; but the objection does not hold

with the elegant adjuncts which the gorgeous ritual of Rome
demands. In the Church of St. Augustine are pleasing groups

Fig. 24.—A Pea-
sant's Cap.

of cherubim and angels bearing floral gifts, that
form the decorations of a confessional (Fig. 27).
Though not absolutely detached from the surface
over which they seem fluttering, they are in
such bold relief, being so much "undercut,"
that the finger may be passed behind many
parts of them. The wood-carvers of the Low
Countries have always been celebrated for their
talent, and their descendants in Belgium still
worthily uphold their fame, as the modern works in Antwerp
Cathedral abundantly prove.

The treasures possessed by the churches in the paintings
which still adorn their walls, and attract visitors from all parts
of the globe, are enormous. Those that chiefly attract attention are the works of Otho Venius (the master of Rubens),
Rubens, and Vandyke. Otho Venius is sometimes termed " the
Flemish Raphael." His works show much of the sweetness
and purity of the great Italian, and are in this way far superior
to those of his renowned pupil; but they are often cold and
formal, and evidence little appreciation of the graces of colour.
Venius was a most diligent painter and designer, imbued with
strong religious mysticism, which shows most in the series
of emblematical engravings he published, typifying the World
and the Spirit. Religious emblems were a book-fashion in
those days, and talented men, clerical and lay, racked their brains

in endeavouring to make the working of the mind take a bodily form. How different from the simple truthfulness of Rubens : his greatest picture, " The Incredulity of St. Thomas," is chiefly remarkable for the unpretentious power of its reality. Here all

Fig. 25.—" Faith : " Church of S. Carlo Borromeo.   Fig. 26.

is dignity and repose. The simple action of the Saviour is excellently rendered, the progress of conviction is admirably traced in the other figures (Fig. 28). You feel that the incredulity of St. Thomas is not quite removed, although he scrutinises with

an earnest, intent, and awe-struck gaze, the wound in the hand
which is extended towards him; but the features, and more
especially the hand, of the younger disciple say as powerfully as
words could do, that he recognises his risen Lord. This simple
majesty and power of expression give a higher character to the
works of Rubens than do their brilliant colouring and masterly

Fig. 27.—From Wood-carving, Church of St. Augustine.

manipulation. The head of St. Simon, in "The Presentation in the
Temple," is magnificent for its dignity and elevation (Fig. 29).
Vandyke's "Ecstasy of St. Augustine" is the nearest approach
to this (Fig. 30). The aged saint, supported by youthful angels
of extreme beauty, is the realisation of saintly humanity. There
is here much grace in the forms, and brilliancy in the colour

of the entire composition, which is certainly one of the painter's best works. The beauty of his angels and younger male figures is again well shown in his picture of the dead Christ in the lap of his mother, now in the Antwerp Museum. A more beautiful group than the two angels and St. John cannot be studied for pathos

Fig. 28.—" The Incredulity of St. Thomas "— Rubens.

and depth of feeling. Nor is the Virgin, with her arms extended transversely, a less speaking figure. She seems truly *accablée de douleur*, raising her imploring eyes toward heaven, as if to seek renewed strength there. The action of the two angels is full of sentiment and dignity—the one gazing on the wounded hand, to which St. John directs his attention with a gesture of affection and

pitying sympathy, while the other, unable to endure the mournful
sight, veils his face in his black drapery (Fig. 31). In the large
Crucifixion by Vandyke (which he gave to the Convent of the

Fig. 29.—St. Simon—
Rubens.

Jacobins in return for the care they took of his
father during his last illness) there is a striking
group at the foot of the cross. The angel is one
of his most graceful figures. The action of
St. Dominic, with his open arms and tenderly
sympathising face, and of St. Catherine of
Sienna, with her closed eyes and delicate
expression of purity, combines the qualities of dignity, grace, and
tenderness, in as high a degree as they can be found in the works
of this great master.

Fig. 30.—"The Ecstasy of St. Augustine"—Vandyke.

It was this power of introducing saintly legend into scriptural
history that gave the earlier artists so much scope for variety

in their compositions, and of which the moderns, for various reasons, cannot avail themselves. When pictures were ordered for churches, it became a necessary duty for the artist thus patronised to introduce the saint to whom the church was dedicated ; no feeling of anachronisms committed was ever allowed to interfere with this arrangement of the subject. This is strikingly shown in

Fig. 31.—Pitying Angels—after Vandyke.

the portion of the picture here given (Fig. 32). The boldest of modern painters would hardly dare to introduce at the foot of the cross saints who are popularly known to have lived many hundred years after that event, and make them take the place of those (St. John and the Magdalen) who are known to have been there. This license gave variety to a hackneyed subject, but it ultimately led to evil effects. Artists were not satisfied with

saintly legend, but emulated classic mythology, and revelled in
groups of angels and genii more fitted for Roman baths (where
they originated) than Christian churches. Some of this false
feeling displays itself in the group: the winged Cupid—for he is
scarcely an angel—seated at the foot of the cross has a reversed
torch beside him, the classic emblem of Death; the lamp and

Fig. 32.—From the Crucifixion, by Vandyke.

skull carry out the same idea. When Art submits to the adoption
of such petty adjuncts, it is a sure sign of innate weakness; the
fascination of such liberty is great, and soon resolves itself into
license; and when weakness and license combine, we get such
furniture pictures as the Church was obliged to be content with in
the seventeenth century, and which sapped the very foundation of

religious art. We see the worst examples of this want of pure religious feeling in the French school of the period of Louis Quinze; but this bad pre-eminence was partially shared by the schools of Italy; it even pervaded sculpture under the guidance of Bernini, whose fluttering draperies emulated pictorial art, deprived sculpture of its innate dignity, and left in place thereof but a miserable exhibition of spasmodic power. The greatest of all Christian temples is disfigured by monstrosities of this kind; we cannot wonder, then, that French sculptors and painters should have been unable to resist the fascination of following in the fashion patronised at the chief sanctuary of their faith.

CHAPTER II.

NTWERP still preserves many buildings, public and private, that existed in that stormy period of the city's history—the era of Spanish rule under the cruel Duke of Alva. Mr. Motley, in his history of the Dutch Republic, has remarked with truth, that no "historic doubter" can possibly take his defence in hand, though they have done that of a Robespierre or a Marat. "Human invention is incapable of outstripping the truth upon this subject. His own letters, and the official records of the Spanish court, are more than enough to prove himself and his master, Philip II., monsters of cold-hearted ferocity." This "most Christian" king, simply because his Protestant subjects objected to the external paraphernalia of his faith, and the introduction of the Spanish Inquisition, devoted a whole country to torture and death. His actions and those of his general "seem almost like a caricature; as a creation of fiction they would seem grotesque;" yet they fill the pages of sober history, compiled from official documents of icy coldness. Indiscriminate massacre or slow torture destroyed hundreds of thousands of Belgic people. When his majesty heard that many had, spite of all torture, declared their faith at the stake, and rejoiced on their road to death, he ordered that they should be gagged, and ultimately that they should be secretly destroyed in the dungeons of their prisons.

The king, who was never seen to smile or be gay, except for a few days, after he received the news of the massacre of St. Bartholo-

Fig. 35.—Prison of the Inquisition.

mew, provided fitting dungeons for his fatal purpose. Follow your guide through the tortuous streets of old Antwerp, and the

gloomy prison may yet be seen (Fig. 33). Its outer doors of solid
oak, strengthened by iron plates, and secured by numerous bolts
(Fig. 34), lead to cells in which imagination sickens. Three are
here represented (Figs. 35—37). The first, of the most usual order,

Fig. 34.—The Prison Door.

is about seven feet high and six feet wide, and is furnished
with a post and chains, with rings to secure the neck, hands, and
feet of the unfortunate prisoner. This has a window a few inches
wide, but many are without, and in suffocating darkness, like the
third, which is fitted for the worst purposes, the dark hole in the

floor opening down into a pit beneath the prisons, whence the
tortured bodies disappeared for ever. The central cell of our

Figs. 35—37.—Dungeons of the Inquisition, Antwerp.

triplicate of horrors is the cell of examination; the post and
chains to which the questioned were affixed, remain (Fig. 38).
The holes in the arched roof will be noticed,
through which the voice of the tortured
ascended to an upper chamber, where the
secretary of " the holy office," with official *sang-
froid*, took down what was said. It is with a
sigh of relief we again reach the fresh air of the
open street, after a visit to such an unwholesome monument of religious hate and cruelty.

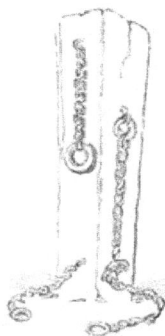

Fig. 38.—In the Prison,
Antwerp.

Externally this building is not without the
picturesque chararacter never unassociated with
mediæval architecture. Numberless quaint houses and picturesque
" bits" reward the pedestrian in Antwerp. " La vielle Boucherie"

is in this category, its quaint character obtaining an additional
charm from the irregularity of its position (Fig. 39). It is one
of the oldest buildings in the town.

We must turn from old buildings, however fascinating, and

Fig. 39.—" La Vielle Boucherie."

study the works of the artist who has given Antwerp an immortal
renown, and which draw towards them the footsteps of art-
pilgrims from all civilised countries. Rubens possessed all a
Fleming's love for pageantry, and was the proper artist for princes.

The wealth of colour and richness of imagination exhibited in his allegorical and historic designs, and some few of his religious pictures,—as " The Adoration of the Magi,"—evince a tendency to gold plate and jewellery, satin, brocade, and velvet. Yet at the proper time he knew how to be tender, even to the tenderness of simple domesticity ; witness his " St. Anne teaching the Virgin to Read" (Fig. 40), a picture remarkable for beauty: the group of angels hovering above them is as bright and fresh as the bunch of

Fig. 40.—" St. Anne "—Rubens.

roses they hold in their hands. This tenderness is still more visible in an episode in that noble picture, " The Elevation of the Cross," the first great public work executed by Rubens after his return from Italy (Fig. 41). Here, amid the groups of terrified and horror-stricken women, stand the Virgin and St. John, their hands locked together as if seeking comfort from mutual sym- pathy. St. John fixes his mournful gaze on his dying Lord ; the Virgin casts a side glance of anguish in that direction—a look full

K

of woe and desolation—as if she could not bear to take in the full sight of the agony which that spectacle presents. These two figures in their sad-coloured and grave drapery give solemn power, artistically, to the whole group. In the picture of "The Dead Christ bewailed by the Virgin" (Fig. 42) there is still greater passion : the head of the Saviour is terribly faithful as a transcript

Fig. 41.—The Virgin and St. John—Rubens.

of death by suffering ; the Virgin averts her head in painful consciousness, with the deep anguish of a mother ; the Magdalen weeps with clenched hands, but her sorrow is without the maternal poignancy. Such pictures may never be painted again : they belong to a past race, like the cathedrals that enshrine them, and which we can now scarcely imitate. There is a deep-seated reflective sorrow in the face of the good centurion as he gazes on his dying Saviour upon the cross (Fig. 43): he leans forward on his horse, abstracted from all other worldly thought, with an attentive, sorrowful gaze. The sorrow of the Magdalen is more poignant (Fig. 44): her extended hands stretched imploringly towards the brutal soldier who is piercing the Saviour's side,

Fig. 42.—The Dead Christ—Rubens.

as if to prevent this last outrage, is one of those touches of nature which go home to the heart.

Rubens is often, and sometimes justly, accused of coarseness in his pictures of martyrdoms. In the gallery at Brussels is a terrible example, in which a saint's tongue is torn from the living mouth. That he was capable of refinement is proved by his treatment of the "Martyrdom of St. John," now in the cathedral at

Malines (Fig. 45). We copy the figure of the saint : the face full of the expression of faith and confidence, looking upward, and upward only, for he casts no thought towards the boiling caldron in which the executioners are placing him.   Irrespective of its

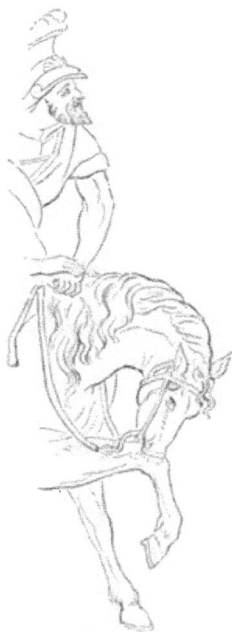

Fig. 43.—The Good Centurion.   Fig. 44.—St. Mary Magdalen.

touching " motive," there is great grace in the *pose* of this figure. In his " Peste d'Alost," there is much of the same quiet grace, as may be seen in the figure we select therefrom.   The expression of trustful hope and resignation in this man as he gazes on the saint is very tender (Fig. 46).

` His great pupil, Vandyke, is second only to his master. In the same cathedral is his version of " The Crucifixion," from which we select the figures of the two thieves. They are as powerfully contrasted as those painted by Rubens in his more celebrated

Fig. 45.—The Martyrdom of St. John.

work. The one on the right of the cross, with distorted features and distended chest, is hopelessly dying in sin (Fig. 47); but the other, over whose cramped and tortured limbs the lassitude of approaching death seems already creeping (so beautifully betokened by the drooping hand which hangs helpless and relaxed over the cross), bears an expression of pleased resignation and humble hope (Fig. 48).

The dead Christ in the arms of his mother, surrounded by weeping angels, is copied from a sketch by Vandyke, formerly in the Van Schamps collection at Ghent. It is remarkable for tenderness, pathos, and grace (Fig. 49).

Malines is happy in the possession of one of the greatest of

Fig. 46.

Rubens's works, "The Miraculous Draught of Fishes." It is one of the brightest, richest, and most brilliant pictures that perhaps ever issued even from his hand. It is full of life and expression, combined with great grace. Witness (Fig. 50) the two disciples who are lifting the net, the younger beckoning to his partners in the other vessel, and the elder intent on the haul; the *pose* of both is admirably conceived; but the idea of the original is wanted to fully comprehend its artistic power. The subordinate parts of this noble picture, the brilliant colours of the various fish, the waves with their foam blowing off in the wind, the sandy beach with its shells, and the bird fluttering over all, are faithful to nature and beautiful as examples of such art-realisations.

The rich store of artistic wealth in these sacred edifices of

Fig. 47.   Fig. 48.

Belgium is astonishing to many money-loving travellers, for they represent large sums, and the fraternities who own them are not always among the richest: but they have an innate love of art, and a pride in the possession of works that can attract men of all countries and creeds toward them. This feeling is not yet fully understood in England, nor the pride with which a Belgian regards the painters of his native land ; it is as if he shared in the

honours the world has awarded them, saying, "I too am a
Belgian," as the enthusiastic master of the olden time exclaimed,
"I too am an artist." It bears the nearest resemblance to the
zeal of the old Italians, who honoured and loved artists more than
they did warriors, statesmen, or princes.

There is still much in these cathedrals and churches, despite

Fig. 49.—From a Sketch by Vandyke.

the fearful havoc once made in them, to remind the spectator of
the days of old. The Romish ritual prides itself on its unchanging
nature; in this country all the appointments of the church
conform to the mediæval standard; and while the Italian church,
with its light operatic music, its theatric decoration, and its

undignified costume, leaves very few solemn impressions on the mind, the great festivals of the Belgian cathedrals possess an innate dignity and grandeur which cannot fail to affect even those who may not adhere to the faith that has called them into existence. There is a regal dignity surrounding these great celebrations, nor is there anything trifling in the conduct of them.

Fig. 50.

The late Mr. Pugin, the architect, than whom no one could be more devoted to his Church, was as honestly unsparing of his sarcasms on the weakness and want of dignity visible in its modern ceremonials and costumes as he was on modern architectural abortions at home and abroad. He has shown, in his admirable "Glossary of Ecclesiastical Costume," how the priestly guise has degenerated from the grandeur of the Middle Ages. In Belgium

L

we may still see costumes as grand as the priestly dresses in the pictures of Titian, or the noble figures of **Loyola, now** one of the greatest pictorial treasures of Warwick **Castle.**

Those who are conversant with early paintings, or with illuminated manuscripts of the same era, which are often very valuable exponents of the manners and customs of past ages, will at once detect the unchanged character of much they will see in

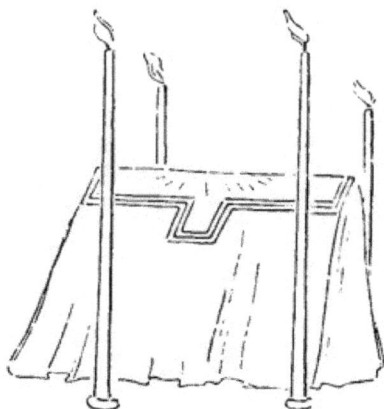

Fig. 51.—A Funeral Bier.

this **interesting country.** We give a small instance merely as a sample of the whole; it is a **funeral bier,** covered with the cross-embroidered pall, and surrounded by tall wax tapers (Fig. 51). It is a sketch of to-day, **but** in no degree differs from one that might have been made in the fourteenth century, so completely identical is every feature of the modern with the ancient style.

The Roman Catholic Church preserved this rigid adherence to

good old forms until the court of Rome became in itself corrupt and careless. The reign of the Borgias was as fatal to manners as to morals. Even in its most solemn, and, we may add, its most cruel ceremonies, the taste of the theatre predominated over that of the Church. Witness the memento of sanguinary old times preserved in the Church of St. Saveur at Bruges (Fig. 52). This faded and time-stained relic is the banner once triumphantly carried before the victims of the Inquisition. The figure of St. Dominic that once surmounted it has decayed by age, and gives place to the crozier, pastoral-staff, and mitre of the archbishop. The central painting represents the adoration of the Virgin and Child by saints and angels: it is mounted on crimson satin, and edged with gold fringe; but it is impossible to look on its faded hues, with the remembrance of its original use, without a shudder, and a grateful feeling that the spread of intelligence among the laity, and the establishment of the printing-press, has, at length, banished for ever such unchristian cruelty from any Church purported to be founded on the words of Him who came to save rather than condemn and who has taught us that "God is love."

In the holier thoughts inspired by these old buildings, in the purer feelings evinced in the works of these old artists, let us walk through the happy and prosperous kingdom of Belgium, with the calm placidity of a philosophic mind. Pictures are to our walls what parterres are to our flower-gardens. To those who look not below the surface, a flower may be a pretty trifle to pluck, to smell, or look at, and cast aside to die; but to a properly constituted mind, like that of our great poet Wordsworth, "a yellow primrose" is infinitely more than so simple a thing as it appears

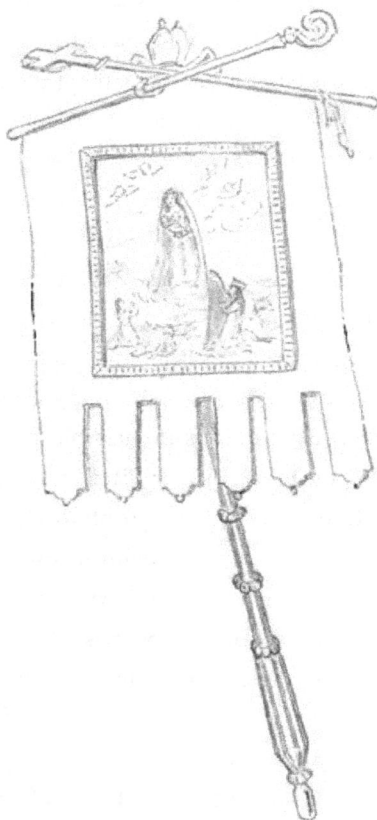

Fig. 52.—The Banner of the Inquisition.

to the unreflective. It was to him "a thing of beauty" in its exquisite colour and form; a "joy for ever" to his mind as a proof of the benignity of the Creator. With some such feeling let us look upon the mental works of the great masters in art, unchanging in a world of change, or even improving as teachers, as time grows older, and the greed of wealth covers us as with a fog-cloud.

In one of the Antwerp churches is a relic of the great painter

Fig. 53.

Rubens, more " personal" in its character than any other the city has to show, if we except the painting-chair which he constantly used in his studio, now preserved in the picture gallery of the town. The Church of St. Jacques required for its altar a new railing, and the rich townsmen each gave something towards a handsome one of bronze. The contribution appears to have amounted to a balustrade each; that given by Rubens is inscribed with his name, and the date of the gift; his coat of arms is also placed in its centre, which we have engraved beside it, on a larger scale, Fig. 53, *b.* The opposite coat (*c*) is that of one of his fellow-contributors, and will remind the reader of the "merchants' marks" often seen in our own churches and on mediæval tombs.

CHAPTER III.

RUSSELS is so happy a combination of the best features of Paris and London, that it has always been a favourite place of residence with the English, who at one time formed a no very inconsiderable portion of its population. Of course the casual visitor goes to Waterloo, though the locality is now much altered since the great day of battle. The continual visit of travellers, making a residence a means of profit, have so much increased the population here of Waterloo and Mont St. Jean, that whereas there used to be a full mile of distance between the two places, the long straggling village of Mont St. Jean is now quite united to Waterloo. We give a sketch of the latter place in its original condition (Fig. 54); the pyramidal mound surmounted by the Belgic lion, commemorating the native soldiery, is three miles off.

Belgium has not many monuments to show connected with its own great civil wars. Outside the gate of Ghent, on the road to Antwerp, are the remains of the tremendous fortress erected by the Emperor Charles V., to check the over turbulent inhabitants of the old city (Fig. 55). Here were imprisoned the Counts Egmont and Horn, and here William the great Prince of Orange led the assault of 1570, when the citizens succeeded in obtaining possession of it, and soon afterwards levelled it with the ground;

the people working as willingly as did the Parisians when they
razed the Bastille; and, like them, being assisted by their wives

Fig. 54.—Waterloo.

and children. Within its boundary is the octagonal Chapel of
St. Macaire. It is enclosed by the heavy ivy-covered walls of the

Fig. 55.—The Old Citadel, Ghent.

central keep (Fig. 56). The cloister of the Gothic Chapel of St.
Bavon, which also stood within the citadel, has much more

picturesque features. It is in the Romanesque style, and was once the centre of the ancient quarter of St. Bavon, whence eight

Fig. 56.—Chapel in the Citadel, Ghent.

hundred houses were removed to make way for this formidable fortress (Figs. 57 and 58).

Fig. 57.—Cloister of the Old Monastery of St. Bavon, Ghent.

Allusion has already been made to the fine specimens of old domestic architecture to be seen in Belgium; they abound in infinite variety. Malines possesses some picturesque examples, of which we engrave one specimen (Fig. 59). Louvain is equally rich, and among them is the remarkable brick building, with geometric tracery over the entire front, given in Fig. 60. At Ghent and at Bruges are equally good, though varied, specimens of the ability of the old Flemish builders.

Many amusing details will attract an observant eye in these old cities. Quaint signs, with their necessary names in broad Flemish, greet passers by. Of these we give four specimens (p. 95). It will be conceded that we use the term "necessary" advisedly, for the "red hound" (of a bright scarlet tint) and "the wild cat" require their proper designations to render them recognisable.

Fig. 58.—Columns at St. Bavon.

The Flemings have always delighted in the grotesque, and in startling popular pageantry. Every city had, and has still, its appointed day of jubilee, generally in honour of its patron saint, when the trade guild parade the streets in fanciful dresses, accompanied by the civic giants, enormous figures of animals, real and imaginary, whales, ships fully rigged and manned, with heathen gods, classic heroes, and heterogeneous characters to marshal the whole. No great city was without its giant, and on great occasions they all assembled to do honour to the advent of some great personage. The only giant who has never travelled beyond the walls of his own city, is Antigon of

Antwerp, and for the most sufficient reason: there is no gate of
the old city tall enough for him to pass under. This enormous

Fig. 59.—Old Mansion at Malines.

figure was constructed in the reign of the Emperor Charles V.
(Fig. 61.) Within the body is a spiral staircase, leading to a
platform on a level with the neck, where a man stands to direct a

windlass to turn the head from side to side when he is drawn on
his car through the streets. He is provided with a wife of equally
gigantic proportion, and a brood of young giants, about ten feet
high, who walk after them (Fig. 62). Their bodies are of wicker-
work, and conceal strong men, who give what vitality they can to
the monsters. They are the delight of the populace, who speak

Fig. 60.—Gothic House at Louvain.

with warm affection of "notre bon père Antigon," "sa belle
Dame," and "nos amiables petits Géants;" yet the history of the
"bon père" would seem to call for no mark of esteem. According
to popular legend he was a cruel giant, who inhabited a castle on
the Scheldt, where Antwerp now stands, and exacted heavy toll
from all boats that passed: if the men did not pay, he cut off

their hands. Braban, one of Julius Cæsar's generals, ultimately conquered him, founded the seignory named Brabant after him, and built Antwerp, giving it that name in memory of the hands cut off (*hand t'worpen*) by the giant, which hands still appear in the city arms, as may be seen in the shield borne by the giant's wife.

Fig. 61.   The Antwerp Giants.   Fig. 62.

In spite, however, of so clear and vivacious a narrative, sober topographers are more inclined to trace the name of the city from its position, "an t'werf" (on the wharf), that led to its great commercial prosperity.

But we must bid adieu to civic legends, and take a last glance at the treasures of pictorial art the old towns enshrine. To begin at the beginning, one of the earliest and most renowned of paintings is still the great feature of the Cathedral of St. Bavon, at Ghent. It is the work of the brothers Hubert and John van Eyck, and possesses all their beauties as well as their faults. The wonderfully sound and brilliant condition of the picture is a testimony to their careful and conscientious work. The principal subject (for it is in many compartments) is "The Adoration of the Holy Lamb," into which design is crowded more than three hundred figures, all finished with the most scrupulous minuteness; that, however,

Fig. 63.—Van Eyck's Virgin.

is a qualification less remarkable than the great degree of character they possess, and the vigour and correctness of their drawing. Larger groups, or single figures, surround this subject. One of the most striking is that of the glorified Madonna (Fig. 63). Her costume is regal, as also is that of the Saviour, who wears the tiara and the golden robes of a worldly sovereign, clasped with jewels across the breast, as shown in our cut (Fig. 64).

Fig. 64.

In the same cathedral are two pictures by an artist very little known, but of great ability—Michael Coxie. There is a series of designs (thirty-three in number) illustrating Apuleus's tale of "Cupid and Psyche," which Vasari says are by him, but which are most usually assigned to Raphael. Coxie is not the only Fleming whose pure love of Italian art would lead connoisseurs to ascribe their works to Italian artists. Otto Venius, the master of Rubens, is often termed by his countrymen the Flemish Raphael, from the character of his designs. The pictures by Coxie in this church represent "Christ bearing His Cross" and

Fig. 65.—The Magdalen, by Michael Coxie.

"The Crucifixion:" from the latter we copy the figure of the Magdalen (Fig. 65).

Bruges abounds in objects of interest, and its old streets and houses are very picturesque; it is, however, so near the sea-coast and the great landing-place, Ostend, that most English travellers, with characteristic impatience, hurry past it. It will well reward examination, as it contains in its churches and public buildings

some of the finest art-works in Belgium. The cathedral (or St.
Saveur, as it is sometimes termed) has a fine picture by an early
artist, Hans Hemling, worthy of Van Eyck; but the great work
of this artist is in the hospital of St. John, whither he had resorted
for cure, after being severely wounded in the battle of Nancy,
1477. The picture was painted in grateful memory of the attention he had received at the hands of the good sisters. Here, also,

Fig. 66.

is the chief glory of his pencil—the famous "Chasse," painted
with the legend of St. Ursula and the virgin martyrs. The
brilliancy and beauty of this work, and its marvellous freshness
after four hundred years, astonish all who see it for the first time.
As a pure specimen of the art of the fifteenth century it may be
said to be unrivalled (Fig. 66).

Wood-sculpture has always been much patronised in the Low

Countries; hence it has assumed a higher character than it generally exhibits elsewhere. We engrave a group from the cathedral (Fig. 67), and a graceful figure of the Madonna, from a

Fig. 67.—In the Cathedral, Bruges.

street corner (Fig. 68). We have already alluded to the interest and beauty that sometimes attaches to these groups intended to attract the pious feelings of pedestrians, and have given some few

specimens from Antwerp; but this group is the most elegant we
have met with.

Near the hospital stands the Church of Notre Dame, a perfect
museum of art.   Nowhere can be seen finer examples of the wood-
carving which has made Belgium famous.   The tombs of the

Fig. 68.—The Madonna at Bruges.

renowned Charles the Bold, Duke of Burgundy, and his daughter
Mary, wife of the Emperor Maximilian, are marvels of design and
execution.   A foundation of marble is overlaid with foliations and
figures in gilt metal-work, and further enriched by coats-of-arms
in brilliant enamel colours.   Funeral pomp could be carried no

further than this, nor is the art-workmanship of the Burgundian era better exhibited than upon these sumptuous mementoes.

The great art-feature of this church, and undoubtedly the finest piece of sculpture in Belgium, is the group of the Virgin and

Fig. 69.—Group attributed to Michael Angelo.

Child in one of the side chapels. It is popularly ascribed to Michael Angelo (Fig. 69), but the fact of its being his work cannot be proved. There is nothing unworthy of the greatest master in its composition and treatment, and it is certainly too good for the best Flemish sculptor, Du Quesnoy. Never was the charm of simplicity more visible than in this work. The dignity of the seated figure greatly adds to the grace of the infant Saviour, the playful and wavy lines of whose position contrast charmingly with the tranquillity and solidity of that given to the Virgin-Mother. Seldom does a sculptured work assert its high place in art more unmistakably than this, the pride of the people of Bruges.

In thus rapidly reviewing the art-labours of a country that has earned for itself so important a position as Belgium, it will be conceded that the difficulties are great, to make all comprehensible in a few pages, and by the simplest anatomy of the subjects treated of, embracing, as they do, architecture, sculpture, and painting. Our task has been lightened by the very truthful sketches—the work of a lady artist—which have helped to make our descriptions clearer, and very often drawn our own attention to peculiar and valuable incidents in a picture. Like the naïve remark that gives piquancy to a narrative, a slight incident in a picture may give it a greater value by an appeal at once to those strong innate feelings implanted in all, and through which "one touch of nature makes the whole world kin." The painter, equally with the poet, has this power; occasionally the painter has the advantage in a more direct and positive form of communicating his ideas. It is the nature, even more than the art, of the painters of the Low Countries, that gives them their position as an original naturalistic school, in opposition to the pure idealists of the Italian school. They have kept their position, and are likely to keep it as long as truthfulness be valued. They cannot take the high rank that by right belongs to the greater artists of the

southern schools; but they do not pretend to dispute that fact, and
are content to rest on their own merits. Sometimes we admire
only their wonderful imitative power, or perfect mastery of the
technicalities of art: but we are often called on to note high
flights of thought and genuine touches of feeling. Where, indeed,
should we look for them, if not in the men who fought the great
fight of liberty and religious freedom in the marshes of Holland
and the plains of Belgium? taught in the severest school of
cruelty and wrong, persecuted for opinion past human endurance,
and quite past modern belief. Keen and deep must have been the
feeling and thought of the Belgians of past times—the noble men
to whom the old world owes a depth of gratitude for crushing the
tyranny of Spain, at a time when that power was vigorously
endeavouring to stamp out with a bloody heel the last hope of
Protestantism.

As a mercantile nation we are also indebted to our Belgian
brethren; they were the first to organise trade regulations and
establish commerce on a proper basis. No one but the student of
mediæval history can form an idea of the absurd restrictions and
the dangers that then surrounded commerce. Protective laws of
the narrowest scope crippled home trade; dangers by land and
water almost destroyed export trade. Cities exacted taxes, so did
nobles, over whose territories merchants passed. If they trusted
their property down rivers like the Danube or the Rhine, they
were liable to the most monstrous exaction, or sometimes utter
confiscation, from the robber-knights who lived in the castles on
their banks, and stopped all passers by for the black-mail that

formed their principal, and sometimes their only income. Honest traders were sometimes incarcerated in dungeons until death set them free, or were tortured for money and robbed of their merchandise. At last the great towns leagued together, promising to aid and defend each other with money and soldiers of their own raising, thus establishing a confederation that soon taught the world the wisdom of commercial laws. The Hanse Towns became most important cities ; the Hanseatic League was found to be of as much, or more value, than royal concessions and chartered promises, often made to be broken. The local government of these towns was another striking feature, and the magnificent *hôtels de ville* erected in all of them testify to the regal spirit exhibited by the merchants of the Middle Ages. Indeed, their pride was sometimes carried far : as when a deputation waited on Charles V., and used their valuable velvet coats, trimmed with costly furs and gold, to sit upon, as the benches were of wood ; the audience over, they rose to depart, and had reached the door, when an attendant came running to remind them of their coats left on the seats behind. " We are not accustomed to carry our cushions away with us," proudly remarked the last of the throng as he passed out of the palace. This pride was doomed to a severe lesson when Alva and his myrmidons came among them ; it was subdued, but never extinguished : subdued in consequence of deep trial, and purer thought, the result thereof; but living still, as we hope it ever will, in the hearts of the brave and free nations of Belgium and Holland.

Our own relations with both countries were at one time most

intimate: "old John of Gaunt, time-honoured Lancaster," was
born in the old citadel of Ghent, which stands in the centre of that
city. By marriage and inheritance our nobility had interests in
the country; by commerce we had much more, and our great

AN DE ROODTE HOND.

Fig. 70.—"The Red Hound.'

AN DE WILDE KAT.

Fig. 71.—"The Wild Cat."

merchantmen were as familiar with the Antwerp Bourse as with
the Royal Exchange. As in London in the olden time signs
hung from every shop, many such signs are still found in Belgium,
examples of which are given in Figs. 70—73. In the days of

AN DE BONTE KOEY.

Fig. 72.—"The Good Cow."

AN DEN CARPER.

Fig. 73.—"The Carp."

Sir Thomas Gresham our merchants had their warehouses
abroad as well as at home; and the houses of the old traders are
still shown at Brussels, Antwerp, and other great mercantile
towns. But as Venice fell by an alteration in the route of traffic

from the East, Antwerp and Belgium generally suffered from the same cause, accelerated there, however, by internal warfare. The greater equalisation of commerce in the present day has changed the exclusiveness that would have become objectionable or dangerous to the various nations; and trade is in general hands instead of a few, resting on its own power rather than on restrictive or protective laws.

In taking our leave of this interesting country, we cannot but recur with much pleasure to the wanderings we have indulged in among the old cities, though we may have felt higher elevation in their picture galleries. Every city has its history, every old house seems to tell a tale. The wanderer in Ghent or Bruges may often meet with an antique street, which seems not to belong to the present time, as if its inhabitants must be only such persons as we see in the marvellous mediæval scenes depicted by their native painter, Leys, of Antwerp. The picture galleries, glorious with the works of the greatest men, possess a rich store, awaiting visitors who will studiously search among them. Art-rambles can be indulged in here second to few in interest, and historic places of matchless renown visited; the days pass quickly and pleasantly during a holiday taken in Belgium; how easily that holiday may be secured by a short transit over the narrow seas that separate her shores from our own, we have shown. History, even our own, connects itself with every town, art with every church or public building "dull must he be of soul" that can ramble in these old cities without deeply feeling the mental advantage he thereby enjoys. It is indeed a privilege to walk where the great men of history, the great men in art, have walked before us ; to realise past history by present things; to re-people the old streets in imagination, with their old inhabitants, when the noble Rubens and the courtly Vandyke gave to the old city of Antwerp a dignity and a glory, which its modern inhabitants, to their great honour, are still proud to acknowledge.

THE MILL AND THE STUDIO OF REMBRANDT.

THE MILL AND THE STUDIO OF REMBRANDT.

N the banks of the Rhine, between the villages of Layor-
dorp and Koukergen, there stood, at the end of the
sixteenth century, a large, old fashioned mill, on ground
slightly elevated, and commanding a less monotonous view than
Holland exhibits in general. It must not be understood, however,
that the Rhine here exhibits any of those features of romance
which give its banks so much attraction higher up the stream; its
flat, unvaried course partakes of the melancholy of extinction as
it divides its water, and, losing itself in the marshy wastes of
Holland, flows into the sea. Herman Gerritz van Rhyn was the
owner of the mill, and on the 15th of December, 1606, the
somewhat gloomy home he inhabited was rendered more joyous
by the birth of a son, who was destined to make the unknown
name of his father immortal. The young Rembrandt van Rhyn
appears to have been left to grow up in boyhood with a perfect
freedom from all restraints, even of an educational kind. It is
reported that he was schooled a little at Leyden, but it is evident
that his attainments could never reflect any honour upon that
seat of learning. Application of such a kind was never to
Rembrandt's taste, and historic research, even when necessary for

the *vraisemblance* of his designs, he openly and avowedly despised. How soon his taste for art developed itself we do not now know, but it is very likely to have been exceedingly early, and the gloomy shade or vivid sunshine which alternated in his

Fig. 74.— Rembrandt's Mill.

father's mill may have impressed his youthful imagination most strongly at a time when the mind is most open to powerful impressions. His early days must have passed somewhat monotonously in his home, which by his own representation had few attractive features.* The mill itself (Fig. 74) seems to be situated over the favourite ditch of a Hollander, which stagnates close by the house, a square gloomy building, with heavy dormer windows, the roof partly overgrown with the rank herbage and parasitical plants of a damp climate. It seems the very realisation of Tennyson's "moated grange;" like that,

"The broken sheds look sad and strange,
Weeded and worn the ancient thatch."

You can detect the marshy moss which "thickly crusted all," while the "sluice with blackened waters" is near, and the distant prospect is but

"The level waste, the rounding grey."

A boy born here, to have become an artist, must have been gifted with a genius for art, and his visible powers for practising it must have been strong to have induced his parents, who appear to have cared little for his mental cultivation, to obtain instruction for their son of its professors. They were not wealthy, and, consequently, could not obtain the best assistance : four mediocre professors of painting are named by Smith in his memoir of Rembrandt as his instructors.† But the very brief period he remained with each, and the small assistance they could have been to him, except as instructors in its simplest rudiments, is

---

* The etching of his father's house and mill, which is here copied, is dated 1641, and was consequently done by the painter when he was thirty-five years of age.

† Prefixed to his complete and excellent "Catalogue Raisonné" of his works.

evident from an acquaintance with their works and his own. He soon left them all, and practised what he knew in his paternal home ; with his taste for *chiar'-oscuro* there can be little doubt that the strong opposition of light and shade constantly before him in the gloomy mill, where his father pursued his avocations, gave him the first hint of the hitherto undeveloped power he possessed, and which he " subsequently carried to such high perfection in his works, that he may be said to have created a new era in painting." * Through life he seems to have always worked as if he had the effect of a small amount of concentrated light before him, and as if every object he portrayed was more or less subjected to that medium only. Burnet, in his "Lectures on Painting," has admirably dissected this principle, as original as it is inapproachable : "in real truth," says Kügler,† "he struggled to give vent to a rude defiance of all *conventional* excellence, and in the fulfilment of this task he has, indeed, produced extraordinary effects. He gives no sharply-defined forms, but merely indicates them with a bold and vigorous brush : the principal points alone are made bright and prominent by striking lights ; but, at the same time, the lights reflected from them penetrate in a wonderful manner the surrounding darkness, to which they thus give life and warmth.

He appears to have reached the age of manhood ere he left his father's roof, and to have had the mill and its neighbourhood for

* Smith's Memoir of Rembrandt.
† "Handbook of Painting," Part II.

his studio, and the boors who lived near for his companions. He never lost his early tastes; and seems to have loved, in more prosperous days, to revert to the lower companionships of his youth. When rallied on this taste in after-life, he honestly owned the little relief he found in high society, or the envied *entrée* he could command to the house of the *élite* of Amsterdam, saying, "If I wish to relax from study, it is not honour, but liberty and ease that I prefer."

How admirably has a great living artist* vindicated and displayed the true position he occupied. "Men of great and original genius, who, like Rembrandt, have little of what is ordinarily called education, and who seem wayward in their tastes and habits, are sometimes looked upon as inspired idiots. But in the mind of such a man, the immense amount of knowledge accumulated by great and silent observation, knowledge of a kind not to be communicated by words, is something wholly inconceivable to the learned merely in books; and if their reading has opened to them a world from which he is shut out, he also lives in a world of his own, equally interesting, the wisdom and enjoyment of which his pencil is constantly employed in communicating to all who have eyes for the sublime aspects of nature, and hearts fitted to receive such impressions through their eyes."

That Rembrandt was thus diligently and usefully studying, is evident from the rapidity of hand and power of expression he

---

* Leslie, in his "Handbook for Young Painters."

P

possessed in after-life. His vigour was untiring, and his industry unbounded. We possess, in Smith's "Catalogue Raisonné," a detailed account of 614 pictures by him, and he assures us that "a list of drawings of perhaps triple the number might be made from the public and private collections in England, France, and Holland;" then add to these his etchings, consisting of 365 pieces, exclusive of the numerous examples of variations in the same plates, and we have an astonishing picture of his powers and industry.

His extraordinary facility of hand is evident in all his works; there is an amusing record of its power in one particular instance, which deserves notice. The painter had gone to pass a day's holiday with his friend Jan Six, the Burgomaster of Amsterdam, at his country house.* The time for dinner had arrived; it was served; but when they had sat down to table, the thoughtless servant had forgotten to obtain any mustard; he was despatched in a hurry to the village close by to obtain it, but Rembrandt, fully aware that to hurry is no characteristic of a Dutch servant, at once wagered with his friend that he would etch the view from the window of the dining room before he returned. The painter had always some plates ready prepared for occasional use at his friend's house, so he took up one, and

---

* The *chef-d'œuvre* in our National Gallery, the cabinet picture, "The Woman taken in Adultery," was painted for the Burgomaster Six, and preserved with scrupulous care by the family until the great revolution at the end of the last century, when it was sold to a French dealer, who again sold it to Angerstein for £5,000.

rapidly sketched upon it the simple view before him, completing it before the domestic returned. Our engraving is a faithful copy of this etching,[*] about one-third of the size of the original; it is dated 1645, and represents the most simple elements of an ordinary Dutch view,—a bridge, a canal, a low, level horizon, a village among trees, with a boat half hidden in the canal beyond. The mark may yet be seen in the original impressions of this

Fig. 75. — Six's Bridge.

rare plate, where Rembrandt tried his etching point before commencing his work, which is executed with the greatest freedom of hand, so that a few lines only expressed the tree and boats,

---

[*] This very rare etching sold in the Verstolk sale at Amsterdam, in 1844, for £17 15s., and would now fetch considerably more, as the value of Rembrandt's etchings has increased yearly.

and a few decisive shadows give solidity and effect to the scene. There is nothing in the etching to dissipate any faith in the tale of its origin, and it is popularly known as "Six's Bridge," or "The Mustard-pot."

At this time the artist was located in Amsterdam: his first recognition as a painter was at the Hague, in 1627, where he had journeyed to sell a picture to an amateur, who astonished him with a payment of 100 florins (£8 6s. 8d.) for it. Houbraken, who relates the story, tells of the joy of the young artist, who travelled from his father's house on foot to his patron, a distance of about ten miles, but was too eager to acquaint his parents with his good fortune to return by the same mode; he therefore mounted the diligence, and when it arrived at Leyden, jumped from the carriage and ran home as quickly as his legs could carry him. In the year following he took up his abode in Amsterdam, and (with the exception of a voyage to Venice, which it is *conjectured* by some of his biographers he may have taken about 1635 *) never left the important capital of Holland.

Amsterdam has been aptly styled a "Dutch Venice;" it is permeated with canals, and founded in the water. It is, perhaps, the most artificial site in the world for a city; being, in fact,

---

* The conjecture is founded solely on the fact of three etchings of oriental heads, bearing the inscription "*Rembrandt Venitiis*." But this, as Smith observes, "may have been a mere caprice of the master," or a jest in connection with his subjects or their treatment, or else a satire on the taste which would prefer the more ambitious school of Italian Art to his own; a feeling fully in accordance with Rembrandt's expressed opinion on other occasions. There is no other indication than this of foreign travel in his life or works.

nothing but bog and loose sand, and every inch of foundation for human habitation or use, has to be made by driving wooden piles through this into the firmer sand below; each pile is formed of a large tree, 40 or 50 feet in length, and it is recorded that upwards of 13,000 were used for the foundations of the town-house alone. This may give an idea of the expense of building in the city, and

Fig. 76.—Distant View of Amsterdam.

the enormous quantity of timber upon which it is constructed, which led Erasmus to jocularly say of its inhabitants, that they, like crows, lived on the tops of trees. The distant view of the town from the Y* side is very curious (Fig. 76), with its tall houses mixed with shipping, some mansions bending portentously forwards, others sinking sideways or backwards, and all showing

---

* The Y or *Ai* is an arm of the Zuyder Zee, which forms the port, and this syllable, or letter, resembles in sound the word used in Holland for water: *het-Y*, the term by which it is usually known, means nothing more than "the water."

the insecure nature of their foundations.* But the most curious feature in the view is the number of windmills mounted on the fortifications on the land side of the town. There are thirty bastions now useless, and upon each of these works windmills are erected, the odd effect of their sails rapidly whirling in the breeze, is a peculiarity as unique as the city itself.† These fortifications now make an agreeable promenade for the inhabitants, the city being built in the shape of a crescent from the water's edge. It is nearly seven miles in circumference, and consists of 95 islands, formed by stacks of houses, to which access is gained by 290 bridges. On the quays are many noble houses, the erections of the rich and powerful merchantmen who, in the palmy days of the city, flourished here. The best bear dates of the days of Rembrandt, and testify to the wealth and taste of their inhabitants. There are a solid dignity and a well-understood comfort about these old houses, very characteristic of that strong domestic attachment which the Dutch so passionately feel. In their love for the substantial they even exceed the English, and the ponderous character of the carved staircases and panelled

---

* In 1822, the enormous corn-warehouses used by the East India Company, loaded with 70,000 cwt. of corn, sank down into the muddy foundation, from the subsidence of the wooden substructure. The old exchange has also sunk, and been demolished.

† Our view is sketched from the borders of the great ship canal, opposite the city, and shows the old church, the quay, and bastions. The boat drawn by a horse is the *trekschuyt*, or travelling boat, used by passengers on canals, consisting of a low covered saloon built in a broad barge, with an open railed platform above, to which passengers may ascend in fine weather.

rooms would more than satisfy the objections of the veriest "John Bull" to flimsiness of construction. Everything seems made as much for posterity as for personal use; and in walking over the town, you see that two centuries have passed over its buildings though located in the dampest position, with scarcely a "defeature" from time, and that they may well last two more. There seems no desire for change in a Hollander; that which is substantial and useful is enough for his requirements, and no idea of modern improvement seems to be sufficient inducement for the trouble of alteration. In walking through the best street of Amsterdam (the Kalverstrasse) you see nothing but the quiet red brick houses, with their "crow-step" gables, that we have been familiar with from childhood in the pictures by native artists; or the heavy wooden shop-fronts, with their ponderous frames, and small squares of glass, much like the old London shops in the prints of the time of William and Mary. There are a few showy shops here, light and airy, *à la Paris;* but they seem to be looked upon rather as superfluous, than a want, by the inhabitants.

One of the oldest and most picturesque buildings in the city, of a public nature, is the Weighing-House, situated near the Museum, and the house where Rembrandt lived. It was originally a gate, before the town had increased to its present unwieldly proportions, and was known as the Gate of St. Anthony (Fig. 77). It is said to have been erected in the latter part of the fifteenth century, and to have played its part in the wars between the inhabitants and their vindictive Spanish rulers. It is a quaint solid old building, and some few years since was used as a

medical school, after its desertion by the merchantmen. In the
open space in front the scaffold used to be erected for criminals,
and others for spectators around it; the burghers at one time
firmly believing such spectacles had their uses in deterring evil-
doing; hence their families and dependants were compelled

Fig. 77. — St. Anthony's Gate, Amsterdam.

to attend these horrible "salutary warnings," as a great moral
lesson.

Rembrandt's industry was untiring, as we have shown, and
appears to have been so far rewarded with success, that he took a
large house in the Blomgracht, and fitted it up for the reception of

pupils. He had married the daughter of a farmer named Uylen-
burg, living at the village of Ransdorp,* in the swampy district
opposite the city, appropriately called Waterland.† His pupils,
according to Sandrart, brought him an income of 2,500 florins per
year, as he received 100 florins from each for that period. His
paintings, drawings, and etchings must have also realised
considerable sums. From 1640 to 1650 appears to be the culmi-
nating point of his genius and his fortune.

Rembrandt's misfortunes commenced with the purchase of the
house delineated in our engraving ‡ (Fig. 78). It was situated in
what was then known as St. Anthony's Bree Street, and which is
now called the Jews' quarter. It was a large handsome mansion
with garden attached, and was freehold. The artist appears not
to have been enabled to purchase it without borrowing the sum
of 4,180 guilders, which was advanced on mortgage; and being
soon after unable to meet his engagements, his entire effects were
seized and sold by order of the magistrates, in July, 1656. The
homeless painter was obliged to lodge where he could, and make
a charge for his necessary maintenance to the bankruptcy court.

---

* The scenery of this village, and the old tower in its centre, were etched by the
painter in 1650.

† By this marriage he had a son, Titus van Rhyn, who, educated for Art, never succeeded beyond copying his father's works, and died in obscurity.—*Smith.*

‡ It is copied from a print published in Smith's "Catalogue Raisonné," from a sketch
by Mr. Albertus Brondgeest, made before the house was destroyed in 1831; the same
gentleman caused a black marble tablet, on which the name of Rembrandt is inscribed, to
be inserted at his expense in front of the new one erected on the site. It is situated at the
back of the museum, the gardens and outbuildings of both joining.

He was but fifty years of age when this happened, but he did not long outlive his altered position, for he is believed to have died in

Fig. 78.—Rembrandt's House.

1664, as his son Titus received the balance from the same court of 6,952 guilders (upwards of £600 English) in the following year, which was paid over to him as a balance of accounts after all claims, including heavy law expenses, had been paid out of his father's property.

From this it appears that Rembrandt, like many other unfortunate persons, was a victim to law and lawyers ; and added another to the long list of men of genius who are fed on by the cunning harpies around them, but who are still ever ready to sneer at the want of business habits displayed by their prey—a sneer too frequently repeated by the wealthier ignorant, always glad to drag

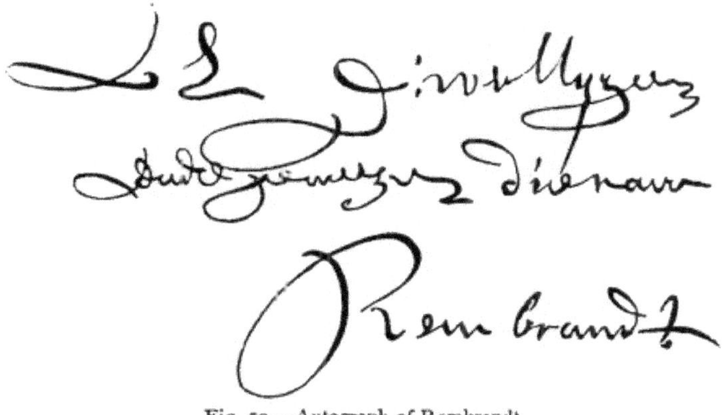

Fig. 79.—Autograph of Rembrandt.

genius down to their own low level. The parsimony attributed to Rembrandt is not unusual with his countrymen in general ; and the stories of his dining off a herring, or a slice of bread and cheese, need excite no wonder in a land where all practise thrift. The fac-simile of his autograph which we engrave is from a letter to the great Huygens, written on a piece of paper which had been previously used to fold round a copper-plate ; but with the artist's little love of trouble, we may account for that by other than parsimonious reasons.* The tales so readily told of the painter's parsimony, and his unworthy tricks in accumulating money, are almost disproved by the melancholy close of his life. Still, at one period he must have earned much. Smith, his best biographer, is inclined to infer that his difficulties resulted from indiscreet

Fig. 80.

conduct in the management of his affairs. Another easy mode of accounting for much loss of cash, is in the suggestion also thrown out in the same work, that the painter's intimacy with Manasseh Ben Israel and Ephraim Bonus may have tempted him to part with his money for alchemical pursuits, as both those persons

* Autographs of Rembrandt are very rare ; four letters in Sloepken's collection sold in London for £33 11s.; the above was in the Donnadieu sale.

were addicted to cabalistic studies, and the former wrote a book on the subject, for which the artist etched four plates remarkable for mysticism. The etching of Faustus in his study, gazing on the mystic *pentapla* which irradiates his gloomy chamber, gives us the best realisation extant of the cabalistic belief of the occult philosophers, and proves how far the artist had studied and was familiar with the dreamy science (Fig. 80).

Rembrandt's scholars were many; but his power of *chiar'-oscuro* did not descend to any of them. Among them were Gerard Dow, Nicholas Maes, and Ferdinand Bol, all excellent in their way, but characterised by few peculiarities like those seen in the works of their early preceptor. Rembrandt cared little for historic proprieties.

The originality and peculiarity of Rembrandt's genius has left him undisputed master of his own walk in art. It would be impossible to improve his faults without injuring his productions. By the magic of his hand he has at times elevated low and disgusting forms into covetable marvels of light and shade : the grand management of pictorial effect is always present, while at times the conception of each picture in its totality is unrivalled in art.

THE COUNTRY OF CUYP.

Fig. 81.—View of Dort.

THE COUNTRY OF CUYP.

IF the accepted characterisation of a nation's felicity, conveyed in the well-known aphorism, "Happy is the country whose history is a blank," may be equally applied to individuals, then may we safely conclude that the old Dutch painters were among the happiest of the sons of Adam. Their lives were generally so entirely void of what playwrights term "incident," that we know little more of them than is conveyed in the three facts—that they were born in Holland; painted in the land of their birth; and were buried very little distant from the spot on which they were born. Contented with the calm monotony of their native land, they studied its narrowed sphere with so intense an application, and delineated it with so much truthfulness, that they imparted a charm to incidents and scenes the most unpromising, and arrested the attention of connoisseurs absorbed in the grander flights of Italian art, compelling, by the innate merits of their work, a place of honour to be assigned the Dutch school, as a creation, *sui generis*, among the honoured of " the world of art."

It is with national painters as it is with national poets, they suffer by translation. It is not possible fully to appreciate Dutch art without visiting the Low Countries. It is not possible fully to feel the beauties of a national poet, unless we put ourselves in the position of his countrymen, and learn to understand the similes he brings from familiar objects, and appreciate their force upon the native mind. The *Ranz des Vaches* may be played in our streets without any other notice than its quaint or pleasing melody elicits; but its tones had so many home-associations for the Swiss soldiers of the armies of Napoleon, that after hearing it they deserted in such numbers as to oblige their imperial master to prohibit it in his camp. The golden sunsets of Cuyp, and the rich green meadows of Paul Potter, can be fully appreciated by any admirer of nature; but the quainter peculiarities of Dutch art—its low, swampy landscapes, sometimes varied by ridges of sand, always abounding in water and sky, with a low horizon, having at times an unnatural look; its cottage roofs scarcely peeping above the raised causeways so laboriously constructed for necessary transit; its stunted willows and avenues of limes; its luxuriant herbage; its thousands of windmills; its well-fed cattle, and equally well-fed peasantry,—are all so many truths, the more forcibly brought to the mind in travelling over the land whose painters have fixed them on canvas for ever, and made them familiar to the whole world.

One instance of this is as good for the purposes of illustration as a hundred would be. In the skies of Wouvermans particularly, we constantly see the bright blue partially obscured by a group of clouds of a perfectly smoky tint—a deep rich brown, totally unlike cloud tints among ourselves, and bearing a disagreeable similarity to our native horror, a " London fog "—now, this is as true a transcript of a Dutch sky, as Ostade's boors are faithful portraits of his countrymen ; and it is impossible to be some hours in Holland without seeing the perfect honesty of many other points in their delineations, which might be considered tasteless or unnatural by the critic who judges at his own home. It, therefore, follows that peculiarly national art can never be fully appreciated out of its country, or by persons who are not familiar with its features ; and it also argues the extraordinary abilities of the native artists of the Dutch school, who could, out of such unattractive and unpromising materials, create a position now universally accorded them, antagonistic as it is to the classic and spiritual schools, which alone were considered to be worthy of attention in the days when it first came fresh upon the world. It was truth again a victor !

Leslie, in his sound and sensible " Handbook for Young Painters," has excellently explained this. He says—" Italy is sometimes called 'the land of poetry;' but Nature impresses the varied sentiments of her varying moods as eloquently on flat meadows and straight canals, as on mountains, valleys, and winding streams; and visits the mill and the cottage with the same splendid phenomena of light and shadow as she does the palace. This was well understood by Cuyp and Ruysdael, and their most impressive pictures are often made out of the fewest and the simplest materials. There is a small sunset by Cuyp in the Dulwich collection. It has not a tree, except in the extreme distance, nor scarcely a bush; but it has one of the finest skies ever painted, and this is enough, for its glow pervades the whole, giving the greatest value to the exquisitely-arranged colour of a near group of cattle, bathing the still water and distance in a flood of mellow light, and turning into golden ornaments a very few scattered weeds and brambles that rise here and there from the broadly-shadowed foreground into the sunshine."

Albert Cuyp was born at Dordrecht (or Dort, as it is usually abbreviated), in the year 1606. It was the year that also gave another of its greatest artists to Holland—the profound master of light and shade, the "gloomy Rembrandt." The father of Cuyp was a landscape painter, but Jacob Gerritz Cuyp never raised his works above a quiet delineation of nature, the simple repose which might satisfy his countrymen, but would never lay claim to attention out of Holland; it was reserved for his son to give poetry to this prose, and by patient stages to work upward to greatness, and slowly to fame;—so slowly, indeed, that death arrested the painter's hand ere he knew the value the world would put upon his labours. In his own time his works can scarcely be said to have been appreciated, and we have no record of even fair prices being given for them; indeed, it is asserted by one of our best authorities,* that down to the year 1750 there is no example of any picture of Cuyp's selling for more than thirty florins, which is about five shillings less than three pounds in English money. How would the worthy painter be astonished if he now saw his works fetching from £500 to £1000 each, and sometimes more! It is the great gift of genius alone to arrest the oblivion which generally follows in the footsteps of time, and, reversing the order of decay, rise triumphant over its common laws.

Cuyp was born in stirring times, when his countrymen were actively engaged in resisting the oppression of Spain. They had not been permitted to enjoy peacefully the unenviable swamps of Holland or the simple faith of their fathers, without a struggle unequalled in the annals of history. The bloody Alva, that fierce and inhuman protector of the Roman Catholic Church, had murdered its men in cold blood, at Leyden and elsewhere, after guaranteed submission to his arms, and their surviving country-men had seen that Spanish oaths were as fragile as reeds; so, after losing the best men of their race, and laying their country beneath water, enduring horrors and miseries which might have been thought impossible among civilised men, they established at Dort a synod which opposed further attempts successfully, and ultimately gave independence to the Dutch.

* Smith, " Catalogue Raisonné."

Dort at this time became the important centre of political negotiation, and here the Stadtholder had his residence, and met those men from whose councils were framed the general independence of the country.* Here resided Barneveldt, one of the purest patriots in an impure age; and here was he arrested and carried to the Hague to die on a scaffold, sacrificed by the very people he had served so well, and who were blindly misled by their treacherous Stadtholder, Prince Maurice. At this time Cuyp was thirteen years of age, and must have been in the way of seeing and hearing much of an exciting kind; indeed, excitement of the strongest was at that time abundant in Holland. Home miseries were, however, succeeded by great successes abroad, and the trade and wealth of the country gradually grew in spite of savage internal dissensions, until the peace of Munster, in 1648, gave over-taxed Holland free leave to recover itself; but they had again the misfortune of a bad governor in William II., who embroiled the country in party war; his death in 1650 once more seemed to promise peace, but growing dissensions arose between England and Holland, and Blake and Van Tromp fought for each country at sea. The death of Van Tromp in 1652, and the gloomy prospects of their trade, induced the Dutch to again

---

* The island on which Dort is situated may be called Holland *proper*, inasmuch as historians inform us it was one of the first settlements made by its earliest ruler on this district, once submerged by the sea, and to which the name *Holt land*, or wooded land, was applied. It thus casually formed a bit of unclaimed land, which gave Count Thierry, who had seized it, a right of independent sovereignty in the eleventh century, which he vigorously upheld, and assisted surrounding districts in doing the same. The water about it is still called Hollands Diep.

apply for peace to Cromwell, which was obtained from him on terms so inglorious that universal discontent and rebellion spread throughout the republic, and increased into a flame during the early part of the reign of our Charles II. The Dutch were aided by Louis XIV., only to meet with his strenuous opposition on the death of Philip IV. of Spain, at a time when the people might have fully expected repose, and a formidable aggression on the part of the French army forced them once more to internecine war ; the sluices were again opened, the country submerged to destroy the invaders, and extensive tracts of land, which had taken years of persevering labour to protect against the sea, were reduced to barrenness and desolation. The murder of the De Witts, in 1672, gave the whole power into the hands of the young Prince of Orange (afterwards our King William III.), who, by his admirable judgment, unflinching courage, and pure patriotism, raised his devoted country from the dust.*

Cuyp lived quietly through all this. The year of his death has not been recorded, but it was certainly after 1672, as his name appears in a list of the burghers of Dort made during that year ; and one writer, Immerzeel, of Amsterdam, states that he was living in 1680. Wars of policy and religion appear not to have affected his calm course. His Holland was not the Holland of

---

* It is recorded of him, that when the proposal was made to him of constructing Holland into a kingdom, of which he was to be sovereign, provided he gave up to England and France what they required, and his consent urged because nothing could save Holland from ruin, he heroically refused, declaring "There is one means which will save me from the sight of my country's ruin—I will die in the last ditch."

feud and dissension, but the calm home of the peasant living
happily among flocks and herds in genial sunshine.

"His soul was like a star, and dwelt apart."

His world was nature, without the baser elements introduced
therein by man ; repose was his treasure ; and his own quiet
temperament is reflected in his portraits, glows upon his canvas
with a warmer radiance, and elevates the scenes he depicts with a
poetry that scarcely belongs to the country itself. It may be
asked, Where, amid all this flatness and apparent monotony of
scene, did Ruysdael study his romantic waterfalls, or Cuyp his
hilly landscapes? The former must have dealt at times in the
imaginative, but Cuyp might readily have strolled from his native
Dort into the province of Guelderlandt, and been among scenes as
far removed from general flatness as he ever depicted. With his
dreamy love of nature, he must have gladly escaped from the political and religious dissensions which agitated that city in his time,
returning to it only as to a workshop wherein he might elaborate
his sketches made in the peaceful fields, and dispose of them at a
moderate rate among his less happy fellow - townsmen. His
patrons are not generally known, with the exception of Prince
Maurice of Nassau, who was attached to his pictures. It is quite
possible that the painter's life was inexpensive and unambitious ;
his pictures would appeal directly to his fellow-citizens and their
neighbours ; and his moderate wants and wishes be amply satisfied by the small amount of patronage they could offer, yet enough

for his small wants and pleasant dreamings as a free man in his native fields.

The visitor to Dort will now see a very different city to that Cuyp inhabited; it has undergone changes, but many of the old buildings remain. As he approaches it by the steamboat from the Moerdyke, he will be struck by the peculiar aspect of the grand canal (Fig. 82). It is walled by dykes, constructed most

Fig. 82.—The Grand Canal, near Dort.

laboriously of earth or clay, and interwoven with a wicker-work of willow-boughs, which has to be continually renewed as it rots away. This accounts for the great cultivation of willows in Holland. The long lines of trees which edge the road on the summit of the dykes have also their uses, irrespective of the pleasant shade their bowering foliage affords, for their roots assist in holding the earth together. So careful of these dykes are the inhabitants, that in some places they will not allow a plant to be plucked by the roots from their sides, for there is record of a great inundation, accompanied with much damage, having ensued by such an act, which gave waterway to a banked canal, the small leakage thus occasioned having rapidly increased, and ended in a torrent which was fatal to the level land near it. The windmills that surround Dort play an important part in ridding the land of superfluous water, which is raised from the low country by their means to the higher embanked canals, and thence carried out to sea when the tide will allow the opening of the great floodgates. The amazing number of windmills in Holland may be accounted for by the fact that they are destined to do at least three times the work they do in other lands. They not only grind grain of all kinds, as with us, but they are extensively employed in sawing wood, and, as we have already stated, still more extensively in drainage. Consequently, wherever there chances to be a rising ground, there a windmill is stationed, and their numbers are sufficient to have quenched the ardour of the knight of La Mancha himself, who must have considered Holland entirely peopled with giants, with whom his single arm could only hopelessly contend.

The traveller who, like Oliver Goldsmith's, would wish to see

"Embosom'd in the deep, where Holland lies,"

would find his quickest course by rail from Antwerp. As soon as he leaves that quaint historic city, he finds the flat land assume a different aspect to the flat lands of Belgium; it is damper and more arid, patches of sand and rushes occasionally appear, and the inroads of the sea in the old times are visible. By the time he reaches the frontier town of Roosendaal (Fig. 83) he will fairly feel that he is in another land. Here, while the most minute inspection of the luggage of the entire train is made by the government officials, he may study the view before him, which we have faithfully recorded in our engraving, and which is as charac-

Fig. 83.—The Village of Roosendaal.

teristic of the country generally as anything he will meet on his journey. The low sand-ridges in the foreground, with a few stunted bushes on them; the higher sand-hills crowned by a windmill; the housetops appearing from the lowland beyond, looking as Hood happily described them, "as if set like onions to shoot up next season;" the masts of the vessels mixed among all,

indicating the presence of a canal in the marsh, too low to
be detected, are all strikingly peculiar features of this unique
country.

Holland being at a lower level than any land on the continent
of Europe, has been reclaimed from the sea by an amount of
labour, in the way of artificial ramparts against its continued
encroachments, unparalleled in the world. Goldsmith has well
described this :—

> " Methinks her patient sons before me stand,
>   Where the broad ocean leans against the land,
>   And, sedulous to stop the coming tide,
>   Lift the tall rampire's artificial pride.
>   Onwards, methinks, and diligently slow,
>   The firm connected bulwark seems to grow ;
>   Spreads its long arms amidst the wat'ry roar,
>   Scoops out an empire, and usurps the shore ;
>   While the pent ocean rising o'er the pile,
>   Sees an amphibious world beneath him smile ;
>   The slow canal, the yellow-blossom'd vale,
>   The willow-tufted bank, the gliding sail,
>   The crowded mart, the cultivated plain,
>   A new creation rescued from his reign."

The necessary expense of this continued strain on the energies
and wealth of the inhabitants, who have constantly to guard
against the dangers by which nature has surrounded them,
renders Holland a very expensive country for residence. The
taxation in every way is immense, and with a national debt
exceeding that of England, the people pay local taxes to a large
amount, while personal property, even furniture, pictures, and
prints, are taxed by yearly rates, increased as every trifle a man
acquires in his home is increased ; hence we find a sordid love of

gain among the middle classes degenerating into downright
cheating among the lower. The stranger visiting Holland must
expect to be "shorn as a lamb," echoing Goldsmith's not very
complimentary lines on the Dutch, following those in the poem
we have just quoted.

On reaching the Moerdyke and embarking in a boat winding
among the large islands known as Overflakke, Beyerland, &c.,
and which seem to have been formed originally by the spreading
currents of the Maas (or Meuse) over the once sandy levels of the
sea, the stranger will more fully understand the amphibious life
of the Dutch—

> "A land that lies at anchor, and is moored,
> In which they do not live, but go abroad."*

With that strange love, born of early associations, a Dutchman
seems to dote on the fetid canals of his infancy; and wherever
the water is most stagnant, and the stench most oppressive, there
he builds his summer-house, and goes in the evening to smoke his
pipe and enjoy himself. How happily has Washington Irving
depicted this abiding trait in his "Knickerbocker!" The Dutchmen of America, true to their home pleasures, repaired to the
dykes "just at those hours when the falling tide had left the beach
uncovered, that they might snuff up the fragrant effluvia of mud
and mire, which, they observed, had a truly wholesome smell, and
reminded them of Holland;" but all this must have been only an
approximation to the real thing, inasmuch as the smell of a

---

* Butler's "Hudibras."

genuine Dutch canal, when its fetid waters are only slightly moved by the heavy, slow-going barges, is something which exceeds description. Yet in these localities do we continually find gaily-painted pleasure-houses, rejoicingly inscribed with words over their portals, such as "Wel tevreden" (well-contented) "Gernstelyk en wel tevreden" (tranquil and content), and others all equally indicative of the content and happiness they produce to their owners.*

Nothing can exceed the vivid colours of the country houses we pass. The brightest of greens, the gayest of reds, the richest of blues cover their surfaces. They are generally separated from the road by the ditches which form a sort of network over the landscape, and the proper way of reaching them is indicated by a wooden door, regularly built up and standing alone—made, in fact, for making's sake—on the edge of the ditch. These advanced gateways are frequently seen in the pictures of Rembrandt, Teniers, and Ostade † (Fig. 84). You cross the wooden bridge and enter the farm. The pasturage, upon which so much depends, is stacked close by the house, and is generally built up round a strong pole, to prevent its dispersion in a stormy wind which sometimes unmercifully sweeps over the flat lands.‡

---

* To the left of our view of Broeck (Fig. 87) there is a good example of one of these erections in a sort of Chinese taste.

† Our engraving represents one near Leyden, which is completely identical with those depicted two centuries ago by the artists named.

‡ In Fig. 85 we have shown this useful and simple mode of stacking, which is universal in Holland.

As they are finished they are surrounded by other poles, supporting a movable roof, which is drawn downward as the stack is consumed, and so it is sheltered while any remains. The farm-house will strike a stranger most forcibly by the solid comforts it exhibits, the rich massive furniture it contains, the looking-glasses in ponderous carved frames, and the heaps of rich old Japanese and other china which abound everywhere,—an evidence of the former trade of the country, once so exclusively

Fig. 84.—A Dutch Farm-gate.

Fig. 85.—Hay-stacks.

and prosperously carried on. The kitchens, with their brightly-scoured kettles, bring to mind the kitchens of Gerard Dow, and the sleek kitchen-maids seem to have sat to Maas for his servant-wenches. But the wonders of the farm are the dairies : here they revel in cleanliness, sprinkling the stalls of the stables with snow-white sand, stroked into a variety of ornamental geometric figures by the broom, when the cows are away ; and when these are present they are as carefully attended to as if they were children, their tails being hung in loose strings to the ceiling, lest they should dabble in the mire! When the cold season sets in, the animals are protected in the fields by a coarse sacking fastened over their backs, much like the coverings here adopted for favourite greyhounds, and the milk-maid is paddled lazily up the stagnant canals that pass round each field in place of our hedges, until she lands on the square patch of swampy grass, achieves her labours, gets into her boat, and is pushed or paddled by a stout swain, pipe in mouth, to the next rectangular plot until her pails are sufficiently filled, when she is pushed gently toward the farm. There is no use in hurrying a Dutchman; he does all things leisurely; anxiety on your part will only make him more perseveringly stolid, and irritation more obstinately immovable.

Town life differs from country life only in the extra gaiety produced by better dwellings, and a greater concourse of people; its formality is as great. The heavy carriages which traverse the streets of Amsterdam upon sledges instead of wheels, drawn by large black horses, are more indicative to a stranger of a funeral than a friendly call. The provision made upon the gabled houses for the board and lodging of the favourite storks (Fig. 86) also indicates the quiet character of the youthful Hollander;* there are no *gamins* here, such as infest the streets of Paris: they could not live many days in this ungenial clime. We can fancy the misery

---

* These nests are constructed on small beams of wood, placed by the inhabitants on their house-ridges, as it is considered *lucky* to induce storks to build. They come regularly to their old nests in their periodical visits, and they are never molested. To kill or injure one would be considered as a sacrilegious act.

of one of them, seized by proper officials, and put into the heavy charity dress, to learn what was proper of a Dutch pedagogue. The lugubrious little old figures that pass for children in pictures of the old native school, seem to have never differed from their parents but in age or size. Formality runs through everything in this land; the night watchman still

" Breaks your rest to tell you what's o'clock ; "

but he does more than this ; he announces his approach by a huge clapper of wood,

Fig. 86.—A Stork's Nest.

which he rattles loudly, probably to warn thieves of his approach, that they may leisurely pack up and go away, and then the guardian, like Dogberry, may " presently call the rest of the watch together, and thank God they are rid of a knave ! "

To see the perfection of Dutch cleanliness or village-life run mad, the stranger should visit the renowned Broeck (Fig. 87), in Waterland, as the district is properly termed in which it is situated. From Amsterdam the grand ship canal, which extends for nearly fifty miles to the Texel, will be seen *en route*, and a four-mile drive deposits the stranger at the entrance of the village. There he must alight and walk over the village, for all carriages and horses are forbidden to enter this paradise of cleanliness. It is recorded that the Emperor Alexander was obliged to take off his shoes before entering a house. A pile of wooden sabots at the

doors testify that usual custom of its inhabitants (Fig. 88).* The
rage for " keeping all tidy " has even carried its inhabitants so far
as to tamper with the dearest of a Dutchman's treasures—his
pipe ; for it is stipulated that he wear over it a wire net-work, to

Fig. 87.—The Village of Broeck.

prevent the ashes from falling on the footpaths ; these are con-

---

* These sabots, once so popularly known by name in England, when it was the custom
to talk of William III. as having saved the nation from " popery, slavery, and wooden
shoes," are generally formed of willow and elm. They are very cheap, and threepence will
purchase a pair of the commonest kind, such as we engrave ; but others are ornamented
with carved bows and buckles, painted black, and smart looking ; these are much dearer,
and worn by the better class of farm-servants, who sometimes protect the foot by a soft
inner shoe of list.

structed of small coloured bricks, arranged in fancy patterns, and are sometimes sanded and swept in forms like those we have described in dairies. Nothing can exceed the brightness of the paint, the polished coloured tiles on the roofs, or the perfect freedom from dirt exhibited by the cottages, which look like wooden Noah's arks in a genteel toy-shop. The people who live in this happy valley are mostly well off in the world, and have made fortunes in trade, retiring here to enjoy Dutch felicity. The pavilion and garden of one rich old clergyman, Mynheer Bakker, has long been a theme of admiration. The good man revelled in

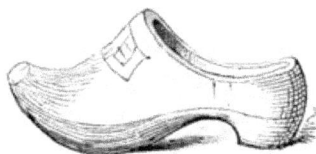

Fig. 88.—A Wooden Shoe.

a caricature of a garden in which he sunk much money; and at his death left a will by which it should be kept up. This is no inexpensive thing in Broeck, for, owing to the boggy nature of the soil, it continually requires attention and renovation.* In this garden are crowded summer-houses and temples of every fanciful style yet "unclassified." Plump Dutch divinities stare at wooden clergymen, who pore over wooden books in sequestered corners; while wooden sportsmen aim at wooden ducks rotting on the stagnant water. The climax of absurdity is reached at a small

---

* The gardener informed us that the surface sunk at the rate of half a foot in a year.

cottage constructed in the garden, to show, as our guide informed us, how the country folks "make the money." You enter, and your guide disappears as rapidly as a Dutchman can, and leaves you to contemplate a well-furnished room, with abundance of crockery, an immense clock, and a well-stored tea-table, at which sit two wooden puppets, as large as life; the old man smoking his pipe, and preparing the flax, which the old woman spins, after the field labours are over. All the movements of these figures are made by clockwork, worked by the invisible gardener, and concealed under the floor. In former times the good lady hummed a song; but her machinery being now out of order, the stranger is only greeted on his entrance by some spasmodic yelps from a grim wooden dog, that always faithfully keeps watch and ward at her feet.

In Broeck no one enters a house by the front door, nor is any one seen at a front window. The front of a house is where the "best parlours" are, which are sacred to cleanliness and solitude. Irving's description of such an apartment is rigidly true: "the mistress and her confidential maid visited it once a week, for the purpose of giving it a thorough cleaning, and putting things to rights; always taking the precaution of leaving their shoes at the door, and entering devoutly on their stocking-feet. After scrubbing the floor, sprinkling it with fine white sand, which was curiously stroked into angles and curves and rhomboids; after washing the windows, rubbing and polishing the furniture, and putting a new bunch of evergreens in the fire-place, the window shutters were again closed to keep out the flies, and the room

carefully locked up till the revolution of time brought round the
weekly cleaning-day." The people of Broeck always enter their

Fig. 89.—Dutch Head-dresses.

houses by back doors, like so many burglars; and to ensure the
front door from unholy approach, the steps leading up to it are
removed, never to be placed there but when three great occasions

Fig. 90.—A Farmer's Wife.

open the mystic gate, and these are births, marriages, and
funerals; so that to enter a Dutchman's house by that way is
indeed an "event."

The country girls generally wear the plain and ugly caps represented in our cuts (Fig. 89); but the richer farmers' daughters, particularly in North Holland, are extremely fond of a display of the precious metals in their head-dress. Pins of gold, to which heavy pendants hang, and elaborated ear-rings frequently appear, and occasionally the hair is overlaid entirely by thin plates of gold covered with lace; the forehead banded

Fig. 91.—A Dutch Road Scene.

with silver richly engraved; bunches of light gold flowers hang at each side of the face, and pins and rosettes are stuck above them. We have engraved a specimen of this oppressive finery, (Fig. 90), which is sometimes further enriched by a few diamonds on the frontlet of the wealthy ladies of Broeck when they appear on a Sunday at church.

It would seem as if a Dutchman really loved the ponderous, for nowhere else may be seen the weighty wooden carriages in which they delight to drive along the country roads; they are solid constructions of timber, elaborately carved and painted, resting on the axles, and never having springs (Fig. 91), which, indeed, are not so essentially necessary as with us, owing to the softness and flatness of the roads. The guide-posts are equally massive, and the outstretched hands with stumpy fingers which point the route to be taken, seem to be made for future generations. The wooden shoes of the peasantry make the foot the most conspicuous part of the body, and ensure slowness; while in some places the horses are provided with a broad patten strapped across the foot, and making their movements as measured and sedate as their masters.* The tenderness with which they look after their beasts, and comb and plait their tails, shows no necessity for a "Society for the Prevention of Cruelty to Animals" in Holland. The solicitude for their cows and pet storks we have already noted; and the number of their charitable institutions is so

Fig. 92.—A Horse-shoe.

great, that poverty or want never meets the eye of a traveller. There is a well-fed comfort pervading all classes, and a scrupulous neatness and order over the whole country, the

---

* The boggy nature of the soil of Holland, and the mischief which might be done by the sinking of a horse's feet, have led to these inventions. The low countries of England can also produce examples of broad protections to prevent a horse from sinking or cutting up the swampy land, somewhat similar to those used in Holland, and which entirely surround the shoe.

result of a constant cheerful industry, which scarcely asks for rest.

It is not the custom of the travelling English to visit Holland; it is a *terra incognita* to them, though other parts of Europe are filled by them to repletion. In these pages we have endeavoured to bring its features strongly before our readers, to enable them, if they will, by aid of pen and pencil, to travel in imagination with us over the land of Cuyp, Rembrandt, and Paul Potter.

THE HOME OF PAUL POTTER.

THE HOME OF PAUL POTTER.

HE Hague has always been considered the most aristocratic and pleasant of Dutch towns. Its old name, Gravenhaage, indicates its position as the boundary of the principality of the ancient Counts of Holland. Its pleasant and healthy position gave it an advantage over most other towns when Holland became a kingdom, and it was chosen as the residence of the court. Its close proximity to the sea, the healthy character of its location, and the fresh beauty of the wood which for ages was allowed to grow as nature pleased in its close vicinage, were all charms uncombined elsewhere, and " *les délices de la Haye* " were spoken of even at the court of Versailles. The palace of the Stadtholder was here, and the picturesque pile of building used as the town-hall was the scene of many an event and discussion vital to the interests of Holland, in an age fruitful of great events to that country, whose annals possess an interest second to those of no other modern European state. It would almost be expected in the nature of things that the marshy tract of unproductive sand which forms this country, would be left to the quiet possession of the industrious people who had with such unwearied assiduity reclaimed it from the sea. Scarcely would it

be possible to mark out a place in the old maps of Europe less
attractive for the foundation of a settlement, presenting greater

Paulus Potter: F.

difficulties to be overcome, and demanding more constant care to
preserve when these difficulties had been conquered.   It was

rescued from the sea only to be reclaimed by it upon the slightest relaxation of vigilant watchfulness; but the fear of encroach-

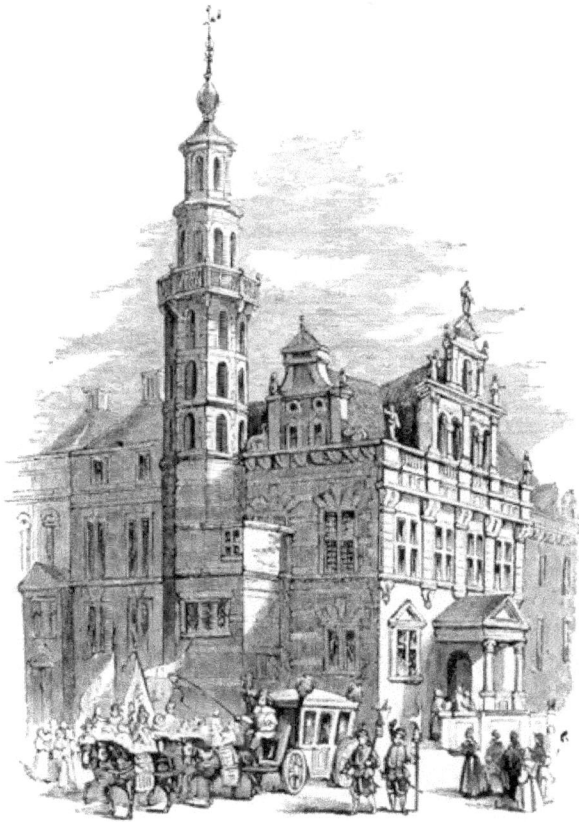

Fig. 94.—Town Hall, the Hague.

ments from their natural enemy was as nothing to the native Hollanders, compared to those which had menaced for many centuries their civil and religious liberties ; and the records of no country present more noble instances of unflinching patriotism and bold love of liberty than theirs do, when its sons were vindicating for its unwholesome swamps the only attractiveness they could ever possess—the consciousness that it was the country of free men.

We have already noted, in the lives of Rembrandt and Cuyp, the quietude with which their days passed amidst the din and bustle of an age of political and religious warfare. In Paul Potter we have another instance of this mental abstraction, which could allow the mind to be withdrawn from the ordinary doings of the world, to pursue a calm course of its own, achieving its own greatness by a placid energy which could not be turned aside from its goal. His life was a short one, but he employed his brief sojourn most earnestly in the study of Art through Nature. He won, and will ever hold, an undying name as its true exponent, while his works increase in value as time adds to their years, and true criticism advances our knowledge. Thus the painting which delighted at first as a simple transcript of nature, becomes, as we study it more, like nature itself—a hidden mine of poetry, awaiting the research of the earnest student who will seek to discover it.

The Hague may be considered as the "home" of Paul Potter, in the best sense of the word—that sense which makes the word convey to the mind all that is genial and lovable, and that marks the happy residence where intellect expands itself freely, and attaches itself fondly to the place of its growth. Though

Amsterdam was the city of his early days, the Hague was the home of his choice, and his happiest years were passed within its boundaries; or in wandering beneath the shade of its neighbouring wood; or seeking subjects in the fertile fields of its vicinity. His desires and wants were bounded by this simple practice, and his native genius could elevate all he saw so readily and well, as to insure a place of honour on the walls of a palace to the simplest rural scene Holland might offer to his inspired pencil.

Paul Potter was born, in the year 1625, in the town of Enkhuysen, where his father practised art, but ranked low as a painter. His ancestors had held honourable posts in that city, and were descended from the noble house of Egmont. Soon after his birth his father went to Amsterdam as a permanent residence, and here he taught his son all that he knew of the rudiments of art. He never had another master, nor did he seem to want one, for his own genius did for him what no master alone could effect; and at fourteen years of age his great ability as an artist was acknowledged; but he felt the trammels of home life, and left it soon afterwards for the Hague.

Holland at this time had declared itself free from foreign yoke; the tyranny, falsehood, and cruelty of Spanish rule had been effectually opposed, even to the partial destruction of the country, and a brighter day dawned on its brave people.* Spain had

* The great dykes, upon which the very existence of the country depends, as already stated at p. 127, were cut in many places to submerge invading armies; and at Leyden, during the memorable siege in 1575, the sea flowed up to the walls of the town, destroying

become weakened in its resources, Germany was torn by religious wars, France was the ally of Holland, while England was busied with its own great civil war, in determined opposition to the encroachments on its liberties made by Charles I. Holland at last held a proud and independent position under its Stadtholder, Prince Frederick Henry. By land its arms had been successful, but at sea they were glorious; and the brilliant victory of Van Tromp, known by the name of the battle of the Downs, from having been fought off the coast of England on the 21st of October, 1639, raised the naval reputation of Holland to the highest point. The trade of the country had steadily increased, and the distant settlements of Brazil and Batavia, as well as the enormous trade with the East and West Indies, enriched the merchants of the land immensely. Although taxation was enormous, and its national debt excessive, the country enjoyed great wealth and power and the taste for pictures and the luxuries of life increased greatly.

The prospects of Potter were therefore good; and the objection made by the rich architect, Balkenende, when he asked his daughter Adrienne in marriage, that he was "only an animal-painter," and ineligible for such an honour, was soon removed by the patronage so profitably enjoyed by the young artist; at the

---

above one thousand Spanish soldiers, the inhabitants sallying out in boats, and continuing an amphibious combat with others who had ascended trees. The whole country for twenty leagues around was ruined for agricultural pursuits for many years. Indeed, during these wars, it became almost reduced to its original state—a tract of waste mud, sand, and stagnant water.

age of twenty-five, Potter therefore married the lady, somewhat gay and flighty for a Dutchwoman, and settled himself in one of the best houses of the town, which was soon frequented by the principal men of Holland, who deluged the painter with commissions, which he executed with untiring energy and comparative ease, because he had in the close vicinity of his home an abundant

Fig 95.—A Dutch Polder.

field of study, and his favourite flocks and herds were ever near him in infinite variety.

The rich character of the vegetation of Holland is due to the irrigation the soil continually receives. The whole country is a network of canals, but it is in " the Polders " (Fig. 95) that the greatest fertility is seen ; this is a technical term for a tract of ground which has been once a morass or lake, below the level of the sea, but which has been reclaimed by clearing away the water. The great lake of Haarlem has recently been converted

X

into most profitable garden and pasture-land in this way. This is done by the simple process of forming a raised bank all round the lake, to prevent water from flowing into it. A series of wind-mills, each working water-wheels, is then erected on this dyke to pump the water upward into a canal on their own level, from whence it is drained off into the sea, or lifted into a series of higher canals by the same wind-agency. Thus we find sometimes three or four stages of canals used to lift the water to a proper level for drainage. The fertile soil which forms the bed of the Polder is laid out into a series of fields in the form of parallelo-grams, each separated on all sides by a deep ditch, the waters in which form the only means of communication with the fields, and render other guard over cattle unnecessary, as they cannot roam from the confined space allotted to them. The small ditches are continually kept to a proper level by the industrious water-mills, and the canals thus filled communicate with the others which intersect the country, and give water-way* for commerce of all kinds, and the supply of the markets. Thus a very large pastoral portion of Holland is artificial, and requires constant watching; the least neglect or inattention might prejudice much property, and ruin an agricultural district.† It has been well observed that

* This simple and convenient mode of transit is abundantly adopted in Holland. It suits the quiet habits of the people best to glide leisurely over the canals from town to town in the *treckschuyt*, or passenger-boat in the summer; while in the winter season the whole population don their skates, and travel with great rapidity over the ice, which affords increased facilities for communication all over the country. Market-women will carry their wares an incredible distance in this way.

† So short a time ago as the year 1825, the whole of Holland was in great danger from

"the inhabitant of the provinces bordering on the sea, or the Rhine, constantly threatened with the danger of submersion, is not more secure than he who dwells on the side of Etna, or at the foot of Vesuvius, with a volcano heaving beneath him. A stranger can have a full impression of this only when he walks at the foot of one of these vast dykes, and hears the roar of the waves on the outside, sixteen or twenty feet higher than his head."* In the days of Potter the system of perfect drainage now seen in Holland had not been introduced ; the small streams were allowed to flow and spread lazily over the land, and the engraving we copy of a Dutch seaport (Fig. 96), from the curious " Book of Emblems," by J. Cats, published at Dort in 1635, gives an excellent idea of this. The sluggish stream which flows from the village inundates the fields irregularly, and men are employed in marking its boggy boundaries by warning-posts. The sea-wall for the protection of the port, formed by the stems of trees, stretches far away, and makes an agreeable promenade. These ramparts are generally formed of clay, their surface sometimes being protected by wicker-work of willow-twigs, which, as they perish in the course of three or four years, require to be constantly watched and renewed.

---

the quantity of water which rushed from the mouths of the Rhine and Meuse, and the extra-ordinary height of the tides. It is declared that had the sea continued to rise but *one quarter of an hour* more, the great dykes which protect Amsterdam would have overflowed, and that city might have been ruined. As it was, it occupied more than two years of incessant labour to repair the damage done.

* The coat of arms of the province of Zealand fancifully alludes to the geographical position it holds, and consists of a lion half submerged in the waves, with the motto, "*Luctor et emergo,*" I struggle to keep above water.

The base, if not protected by piles, is generally faced with stones,
or walled with hard-baked bricks, called clinkers, while rows of
piles form breakwaters as a further protection to their solidity.
Thus continuously has the Hollander to labour in the preservation
of his country, and nowhere is industry so strikingly visible as
among the Dutch; for it meets the eye continually, and challenges
observation everywhere. The ground beneath the feet is " made

Fig. 96.— A Dutch Seaport : 1635.

earth," to use a gardener's term ; sometimes brought from considerable distances, and only preserved from being washed away
by the embankments just alluded to. This necessary attention to
the state of the land produces an extremely *artificial* look over its
entire surface. It seems as if the whole country had been
constructed by human labour ; more particularly as the Hollander
scarcely allows a blade of grass to grow freely—all is trimmed
and tended with care ; while bushes and shrubs are subjected to

the gardener's shears, and cut into those wonderful figures of birds and beasts occasionally to be seen in quiet English villages, where Dutch taste has penetrated.* Even large trees occasionally assume the form of square masses of foliage supported on naked upright stems, or else are tortured on iron frameworks till they look as little like trees as a Chinese lady's foot resembles that of the Venus de Medicis.

In Holland the laws of nature seem to be reversed; the sea is higher than the land—the lowest ground in the country is 24 feet below high-water mark, and when the tide is driven high by the wind, 30 feet! In no other country do the keels of the ships float above the chimneys of the houses, and nowhere else does the frog, croaking from among the bulrushes, look down upon the swallow on the house-top. Where rivers take their course, it is not in beds of their own choosing; they are compelled to pass through canals, and are confined within fixed bounds by the stupendous mounds imposed on them by human art, which has also succeeded in overcoming the "everywhere-else" resistless impetuosity of the ocean. In a very extensive range of the country there is not a stone or pebble to be found in the alluvial or sandy soil; and there are no hills, save such as are raised by the winds; unless, indeed, we take into consideration those vast artificial mountains of granite which have been brought at enormous expense from Norway and Sweden, and sunk under water to serve as barriers to the sea. Excepting the eastern provinces, the parks of

* See subsequent article, "The Dutch Landscape and Flower-Painters."

Haarlem and the Hague, and the avenues leading from one city to another, the land does not produce much wood; but then entire Norwegian forests have been buried beneath the mud in the shape of piles.[*]

It is in some degree surprising that so pure and good a school of natural art should have been formed by its native-born painters, and still more remarkable that men thus compelled to see only conventional views of nature's beauties, should look upon the goddess dressed in Dutch taste, but delineate her in all the freedom of the purest innocence and simplicity. We might have expected a sort of Chinese landscape painting to have predominated, and cattle to have rivalled in pictures the productions of their own pottery at Delft; but the painters of Holland never committed this error, they seem to have avoided with scrupulous care any other than the purest features nature presented to them. To them she denied her grander traits—the rocky beauties of Switzerland, or the verdant graces of Italy. With them the all-glorious Rhine became a flat heavy stream, pouring its many mouths to the sea in a swamp of mud; yet limited as the field of native art thus necessarily became, the Dutch artists, by their unwearied study of nature, and profound and patient delineation of its most minute characteristics, founded a school at once original and excellent.

Among all their national painters, none held higher rank than Paul Potter, whose finest work, "The Young Bull," still

* Murray's "Handbook for Holland."

decorates the public gallery of the Hague, the favourite residence of the painter, the scene of his studies and his triumphs, but wanting, alas! in the greatest joy of all—domestic felicity. His wife was fond of flirtations, which gave the peaceful painter constant uneasiness, and to such an extreme was this at last carried, that the artist one day caught his wife listening to one of her admirers; when, enraged beyond measure, he cast over them the net-work he carried on his arm, and which he had taken from his horse, who wore it to keep off the flies; then tying them together with it, he exposed them both to the laughter of the friends in his house. So ridiculous and disgraceful an affair soon became the talk of the town, and at last grew to be so disagreeable as to oblige the painter to remove to Amsterdam.

It was in 1652 that the painter settled in that city. The Burgomaster Tulp was his great patron, and enriched his fine gallery with the principal works of the artist. Amsterdam was at this period one of the wealthiest of European cities, and its rich traders delighted in embellishing their houses with pictures, carvings, and the rarest and most costly works of India, China, and Japan—a taste which has survived to the present day; and nowhere is so much of the finest work of this kind to be seen as in Holland, while rare old china is in the dealers' shops as common as Staffordshire ware among ourselves. The noble old houses of Antwerp, constructed by the De Ruyters, the Van Tulps, and the rich burghers of old days, still stand to attest their wealth and magnificence; but if we would see the city as in the days of its greatest glory, we must turn over the pages

of the chroniclers of its great public events. There is a
magnificent volume devoted to a detail of the reception given
by the city to Catherine de Medicis, embellished by the most
minute and beautiful engravings by Savery, and we have
selected a view on the grand canal (Fig. 97) from this rare volume,
to illustrate the Amsterdam of Potter's era.* The view comprises a group of imposing houses, intersected by smaller canals,
over which miniature bridges are carried, and it gives an
excellent idea of the characteristics of one of the most extraordinary cities of Europe. Some few of these noble mansions
still remain in Amsterdam in all their pristine integrity, giving
a stately look to its old quays as their time-honoured fronts
surmount the trees which line the borders of the canals. Their
architectural characteristics might be considered as "debased"
in the judgment of a severe student of architecture; but they
have an imposing effect with their rich arcades, floriated
pilasters, and fanciful gabled fronts, surmounted by statues or
vases of flowers.

After the removal of Potter to Amsterdam, he enlarged the
proportions of his pictures, forgetful of the important fact that
size does not constitute greatness—for the ancient artists of
Greece developed their genius as grandly upon an intaglio or
a coin as they did upon the Elgin marbles. He was, in fact,

---

* It is entitled "Blyde Inkomst der Allerdoorlughtighste Koninginne Maria de'
Medici t'Amsterdam," and was published in that city in 1639; her majesty having paid
the visit on her way to England, to visit her daughter, Henrietta-Maria, wife of our Charles I.

betrayed into this by emulation rather than design, for he saw
there, in the possession of wealthy amateurs, pictures of far
larger proportions than he had been in the habit of painting,
and he was anxious that size should be no bar to his success.

Fig. 97.—Amsterdam in 1639.

The life-sized pictures of animals he now painted, although
characterised by vigour and truth of touch, lose greatly in
interest and beauty by their gigantic proportions, and the
celebrated bull at the Hague disappoints at first sight, while

Y

few would wish to possess it in preference to his less obtrusive works. But to whatever scale the artist worked, he was always the captivating exponent of simple nature, and gave a truth, and a life, and a poetry to his scenes, which elevate the commonplace to the classic.

An early death awaited the artist; he had not completed his twenty-ninth year when he expired of a decline, leaving behind him the wife he fondly loved, in spite of her blamable levities, and a little daughter three years old. In the great chapel at Amsterdam (Fig. 98) lie the remains of Paul Potter, one of the greatest artists of Holland. He reposes in the very reverse of the quiet scenes he loved so well to depict. All around is the bustle of life, the throng of commerce, the din of busy feet. The quaint and characteristic steeple peeps over tall warehouses, surrounding busy docks where produce is unladen from all quarters of the world. You cannot rest on the bridges which span the canal to reflect on the mausoleum of the painter, for the heavily-laden cart is constantly moving with merchandise, or the quaint old coach almost noiselessly sliding on its sledge in place of wheels, might too dangerously disturb your reverie. There is something incongruous in seeking the grave of the pastoral painter in such ungenial scenes ; and in the very midst of " life's fitful fever" to find the grave of one who revelled in " fresh fields and pastures new;" who studied them with a poet's love, and delineated them with the highest artistic power ; whose whole soul was imbued with a love of nature, and who should have slept where trees shadow and flowers garnish the sod.

An artist like Potter is a *creator* of a style; his genius enables him not only to delineate what he sees, but to express the hidden sentiment which gives the charm to nature itself. He has gone below the surface. He has been thus contrasted with painters of his school by a modern critic: "Others have painted

Fig. 96.—The Great Chapel, Amsterdam.

cows, oxen, well-drawn sheep, all well-coloured and painted. He alone has seized their expression, the physiognomy of their inner existence, of their instinct. We admire the flocks and herds of Berghem, of Van der Velde, of Karel Dujardin; we are touched by those of Paul Potter."

It should ever be remembered that it is to the artists of

Holland we owe a relief from the trammels of the mere "academic" school. It is to their love of nature, and persevering study of her beauties that we are indebted for a purely natural series of pictures, which rely alone for immortality on their true reflection of her varied beauties. The world as it lay around us was long a book unstudied in the flights of fancy after the ideal. To them was given the power of discovering the gold that is hidden amid the dross; the poetry that is in humble nature; the sentiment that lurks beneath the simplest form. They *created* therefore a new school of art, and a school which might successfully appeal to all, by the simplicity of its sphere of action. The minute traits of nature in their pictures resemble the charming traits of her features which delight us in the poetry of Shakspere or of Burns. As the "lush woodbine" or the "mountain daisy" could gladden the hearts of these noble poets into song, so the changing aspects of the sky could elevate into grandeur the simplest elements of Rembrandt's pictures, and the level meads and happy cattle of Paul Potter give a sentiment of happiness to the spectator, like that felt by Goethe's "Faust," when, tired of all the artificial glories of life, he feels his loftiest emotions arise from the contemplation of the fertile fields and happy peasantry around him. Truly

"One touch of Nature makes the whole world kin,"

and while this cosmopolitan relationship exists the Dutch painters will find admirers.

THE DUTCH GENRE-PAINTERS.

THE DUTCH GENRE-PAINTERS.

THE Hollander, as represented by his own native artists, is as distinct from the rest of the *genus homo* as the style adopted by the hands which have immortalised his peculiarities. He is known everywhere—by the rich connoisseur who glories in the possession of the original works of Ostade, Gerard Douw, Brauwer, or Jan Steen ; and by the poorer lover of art, in the many copies produced by the facile hand of the engraver. The entire truth of these pictures, and their quaint originality, thus enforce full claim upon attention, even when divested of the charm of colour. Well, then, may the wealthy collector of taste rejoice in the possession of genuine works so remarkable for both qualities as are the pictures by the painters of the Netherlands. With them originated that peculiar choice of subject from ordinary life which has received the *soubriquet* of *genre-painting*, from the impossibility of classing it with the grander imaginings of the Italian school. Art was in that school principally devoted to the sacred service of the Church, or the dignified realisation of historic scenes ; it therefore always possessed a certain elevated dignity when it approached ordinary life in portraiture ; but in no instance did

it free itself from conventional or scholastic education, and give
itself up to the delineation of everyday life with the zest of

an Ostade, who would bestow all the graces of art on an old
woman threading her needle; or with the dashing joviality of
Jan Steen, who would revel in a tavern scene with greater gusto

than had ever been seen before in the history of imitative art.
Their success as a school produced a revolution in the general
canons of criticism, and the ability displayed in their works
asserted a position for a new body of painters then struggling
into notoriety, who, discarding the *grandiose* (by this time become
a little absurd from the scholastic tendencies of its devotees,
who too frequently indulged in mixing the real and the fanciful,
the present world with the past, history and mythology in unreal
conjunction), placed their starting-point in Nature alone, making
her works the limit of their studies, and bringing only the graces
of art to the proper adornment of what she placed before them—
believing no created thing unworthy their earnest attention, and
no attention ill-bestowed that could present it to their fellow-men
surrounded by all the artistic graces consistent knowledge could
bring to bear on its delineation.

This term *genre*, was applied somewhat scornfully by the
French critics, in the days of the *Grand Monarque*, to designate a
school of art they could not comprehend, and which they chose to
consider as out of the pale of art-proper, or rather the art of
Versailles. Louis XIV. would never admit a Dutch picture into
his galleries, which were, however, open to the travesties of
Scripture subjects his native artists painted with so much
complacency, as well as to the theatrical flutterings of Bernini's
sculpture. The grandiose trifling, which then passed for dignity,
and the constrained manners which made up an etiquette as
wearisome as if it were Chinese, gave no scope for the minds
nurtured in formal conventionalities to understand the charm of

z

simplicity or Nature. The lowest grade of a true art takes higher stand than the art produced in the hotbeds of the French court, nurtured under unnatural auspices : its despised products have passed away like all other "whims of a day," but the greater works of the honest Dutchmen remain.

Though Ostade is inseparable from Dutch art, and by his genius was the earliest to raise it to renown, he was not a native of the country. He was born at Lübeck, in Germany, in 1610. Hence some biographers unhesitatingly place him among German artists; but he was unquestionably German only by the accident of birth ; for abandoning his native country early in life, the formation of his mind and the knowledge of art he possessed were essentially Dutch. Like many a foreigner undergoing the change of thought and habit produced by a residence among strangers, he became ultimately more national than the native born, and earnestly devoted his ability to the delineation of the people of his choice with a zest and power hitherto unknown. Holland did not in his time want for wealthy amateurs, and, although the long life of Ostade was spent amid political turmoil, the country was improving in wealth and importance beneath the rule of great public men. It is to Frank Hals, of Haarlem, that he was indebted for the knowledge he obtained of the mere manipulation of art. Frank was a free, dashing painter, but a perfect tradesman in his profession. He had considerable tact in producing saleable pictures, and also in discovering young and needy men of genius who would aid him in multiplying them quickly. His wife, as avaricious as himself, fostered the

trading spirit, and between them they made the studio a mere
shop, and the pupils mere mechanics. At the time Ostade was in
this state of servitude he had as a fellow-pupil Adrian Brauwer,
with whom Hals had accidentally become acquainted, and whose
ability he had detected in the humblest employ. His mother
was a poor milliner at Haarlem, and he used to sketch on paper
for her the flowers and other ornaments with which she
embroidered the caps and collars of her customers. The ability
shown by the boy in designing these decorations induced Hals to
examine his sketches, and ask if he would like to be a painter.
The boy readily replied in the affirmative. His mother was
consulted on the subject, but she would agree only on condition
that Hals should entirely provide for him during his pupilage.
He consented; but, with wretched parsimony, when he found
the lad's ability, locked him in a wretched garret, and made him
labour continuously with hardly sufficient food, without money,
and without relaxation. His fellow-students, however, behaved
more mercifully by him, and commissioned him to make them
sketches for a few pence each in such few moments as he could
snatch for that purpose. His master discovered this, and
punished the poor lad by making him work harder on still less
food, until, persecuted more than nature could bear, he broke
from his prison and escaped. With the childish experiences of a
boy, he made provision for the first day of his liberty by
purchasing as much gingerbread as he could carry in his pockets;
and then ensconcing himself beneath the carved case of the
famous great organ in the principal church of the town, leisurely

enjoyed this delicacy. After a few hours his situation became irksome; he was lonelier than in Hals's studio, for his artistic implements were wanting; hunger, too, outmatched his ginger-bread, and he ventured forth ruefully to the church porch. Here he was recognised by a passer-by, who had known him in his master's house; from the poor boy he learned his melancholy story, and at once offered to be the mediator between them— succeeding so well that Hals behaved better to him; for he was anxious to profit by his genius, and had sold many of his works at high prices, as the production of a foreign artist of great merit.

It was at this time that Ostade came into Hals's studio as a pupil, and fully appreciating Brauwer's ability, and indignant at the manner in which he was treated, urged him to try his fortune on his own account, and escape to Amsterdam, which was then full of connoisseurs. Brauwer took his advice, and luckily went on his arrival to an inn kept by one Van Sommeran, who had been a painter in early life, and whose son still practised the art. Here he was well received, and his talent appreciated. It was soon discovered by an amateur, to whom his first picture was shown, that he was the "foreign artist" whose works Hals had sold so highly. He was well-paid for his work, and became, from the depth of poverty and privation, free and comparatively rich. It is little to be wondered at that he revelled in the change. He gave himself up to tavern life, painted sottish scenes, and the rude brawls they engendered, and spent his money among the drunken boors he painted—

caring little to work before it became absolutely necessary to obtain money for his creditors.

Ostade, possessed of true German phlegm, went on a steadier course. Disgusted with his master, he quietly abandoned him, but settled down beside him in the city of Haarlem to obtain honestly patronage for his own talents. He tried them in various ways; but being a young and inexperienced man, he fledged his wings in imitative art, and endeavoured to rival the works of Rembrandt and Teniers. He did not succeed; yet he did not fully feel his own power of originality until his old fellow-pupil Brauwer paid him a friendly visit, and urged him to throw away conventionalities, and depend on the strength of his own genius. The hearty advice of the grateful young painter, to whom he had once tendered advice as useful, determined his course, and he struck out a style which has invested his pictures with a charm all his own.

Unlike Brauwer, Ostade was a quiet, industrious man. He married the daughter of Van Goyen, the marine-painter, and a large family was the result of the union, for whose support he laboured unceasingly until the necessity for improving his monetary affairs induced him to make a change, and he decided on returning to his native town to settle there; but he got no farther on his road than Amsterdam, where he found so much patronage, that about the year 1662 he settled there, making the neighbouring villages the scenes of his study; and, with the characteristic quietude of his life, having found out his *forte*, a fair field for study, and a due amount of patronage, he never left Amsterdam ; and died among his patrons in 1685, at the ripe age of seventy-five.

In his pictures we see the best transcript of Dutch life in that era : the happier and better class of subject was chosen for his delineation. The tavern brawls, the drunken orgy, or the coarse village fête, had no charms for his pencil ; but the rustic at home amid his family, or enjoying himself with his pipe, or listening over the trellis-hung door of his cottage to the travelling minstrel's simple melody, often employed his pencil, as is seen in the example here given (Fig. 100). He never caricatures their simple life ; and, while displaying it in the most complete homeliness of its character, never offends by want of taste, however low the grade of the persons he may represent. Poor though they may be, they are seldom repulsive, as in many of the works of the artists of the Low Countries ; while the heartiness of their joy as they look on their children, or revel in the simple pleasures they can obtain, gives them an interest and a claim on attention that pure honesty always may command. They show how much poetry there is in common things, and how much lurks beneath

"The short and simple annals of the poor."

The life of Brauwer possesses great stirring interest ; indeed, it may be said to be the most eventful career led by any Dutch painter. They generally passed through their course of life so quietly and simply, so industriously and prosperously, that we know little more of them than that they lived, painted, and died. The adventurous spirit of Brauwer, and the erratic

Fig. 100.

nature of his tastes, led him into a more chequered path. Cradled in poverty, a slave to a bad master, as he emerged to manhood he ran a reckless course, when liberty and money came into his possession. He must have been occasionally taken for a madman by his stolid countrymen. Many are the quaint

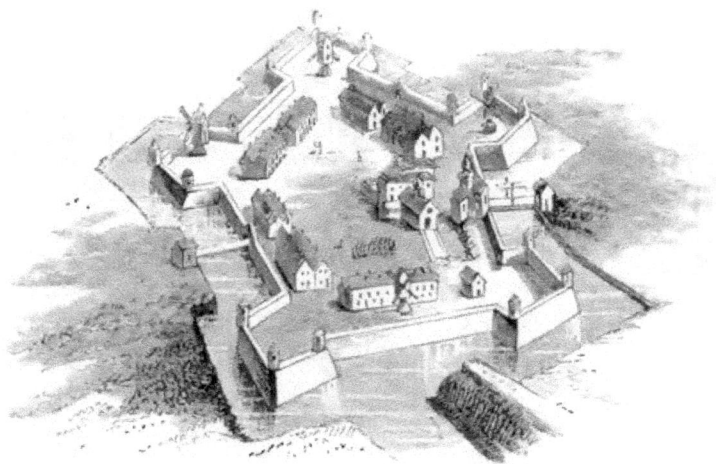

Fig. 101.—The Citadel of Antwerp in 1603.

stories told of the painter—his recklessness and his buffooneries, which must have frequently set the tavern in a roar. He had much caustic humour also; and it is narrated of him, that being invited to a wedding, and feeling it was only because he had discarded the slatternly clothes he usually wore, and donned a suit of velvet, he soaked his new coat in the richest sauces on the table, declaring that the good cheer could only be properly bestowed on the thing invited; and then casting it on the fire, he coolly walked back to his old tavern companions. Immersed in his studies of low life, and enjoying only such scenes as he loved to paint, he never sought to amass money; and it is recorded of him, that on one occasion, when a considerable sum was paid him, he abandoned his pencil and home for nine days, until he had spent it all, returning penniless, and praising heaven that he had at last got rid of it.

This reckless life naturally produced the usual bad results, even to a man of so few wants as Brauwer. His debts accumulated, and at last were so portentous that he saw no escape from his liabilities but flight. He left Amsterdam, and hurried to Antwerp; but when he reached that city he was at once arrested by the soldiery, for the thoughtless painter had no passport, and the Hollanders were waging fierce war against the Spaniards, who claimed to be their governors, and in whose hands Antwerp was held. He was at once marched to the citadel* (Fig. 101) as a Dutch spy, and in it encountered the Duke d'Aremberg, who was imprisoned there by order of the Spanish king, and whom the painter imagined to be the governor of the fortress. In profound tribulation Brauwer told his simple tale, and assured him he was only a poor painter. To test his story, the duke

---

* Our engraving exhibits the aspect of the citadel of Antwerp at the time when the painter was prisoner there; it is now a much stronger position. In his time it was fed by a canal connected with the Scheldt, and the ramparts economically served the purpose of foundations for windmills to grind the corn of the garrison. The necessary houses for troops are arranged with Dutch formality; a chapel is also contained within its bounds, and an open space for the exercise of the soldiery. It was constructed by the celebrated engineer, Pacciotti, that the cruel Duke of Alva might overawe the men of Antwerp.

A A

good-naturedly sent a messenger to Rubens, then residing close
by, and obtained from him canvas and colours for Brauwer,
who at once set to work, and painted a group of soldiers who
were engaged beneath his prison window in a game of cards.
When it was finished it was shown to Rubens, who at once
declared it to be a work of Brauwer's. That really great and
generous man went immediately to the governor, begged for the
liberty of his fellow-artist, and ultimately obtained it on
becoming personally answerable for his conduct. He did not
rest here; but took Brauwer to his own princely mansion in
Antwerp, where he gave him a chamber for his exclusive use,
clothed him anew, and assigned him a place at his table.

Fortune now seemed to have done her best for Brauwer,
but he was not the man to value her smiles. His short residence
in the house of the courtly Rubens, who lived more like a prince
than a painter, instead of elevating only depressed a man whose
chief joy centred in tavern life. Like old Walter Mapes, his
aspiration was—

> "In a tavern to be till the day of his death,
>   With no stint to the full-flowing bowl,
> That angels might sing, as he drew his last breath,
>   'Rest and peace be to this thirsty soul.'" *

---

* Walter Mapes flourished in the twelfth century as Archdeacon of Oxford. This
thirsty churchman thus expressed himself in the first stanza of his celebrated convivial song,
with a strength above our translation—

> "Mihi est propositum in taberna mori,
>   Vinum sit appositum morientis ori,
> Ut dicant, cum venerint angelorum chori,
>   'Deus sit propitius huic potatori.'"

He made a precipitate retreat from Rubens' house to the beershops, selling his clothes for drink. Becoming acquainted with a boon-companion, one Joseph van Craesbeck, a baker, he took the offer he gave the painter to board and lodge him on condition that he gave him lessons in art. Master and pupil were as constantly carousing as painting, until at last all things

Fig. 102.—Gate of St. Julian's Hospital, Antwerp.

went so ill with them that flight was again necessary, and both started for Paris. Brauwer, however, found the life of the Parisian unlike the beer-drinking of Belgium and Holland, and longed to return. But he got no farther on his road back than Antwerp, where he arrived, suffering from disease, exhaustion, and neglect. As a pauper he was received in the old public hospital of the city (Fig. 102), and there died wretchedly, in the year 1660.* His body, wrapped in the straw pallet upon which he died, was inhumed in the burial-ground devoted to the plague-stricken ; but his old friend Rubens, hearing of this, and much moved at the untimely end of so true a genius and so great an artist, had him re-buried at his own cost, with all honour, in one of the principal churches of the city, and determined to erect a monument to his memory. He perfected his design, but was himself numbered among the dead ere he could have it executed.

In Gerard Douw we find the quietude of an Ostade. Throughout a long life he resided at Leyden (Fig. 103), and devoted his whole thought to his art. Painstaking in a most extraordinary degree, he laboured unremittingly on his pictures ; and Sandraat, in recording a visit he paid him in company with Bamboccio, narrates, that Douw declared he should bestow three days more in finishing a broom in one corner of the picture, which had already attracted the attention of both by its laborious manipulation. In all his works he indulged the same love of minute finish ; and he was as careful of the colours he used, grinding them himself, and treading his studio on tiptoe, lest he should raise dust on his palette to injure their brilliancy. The richness and purity of his colouring are still unrivalled ; and though with some painters such extreme love of minute finish

* The public hospital of Antwerp is appropriately named after St. Julian, that saint being the patron of travellers. It is still a large and useful establishment, but preserves no traces of its antique features except the old Gothic doorway given above.

might sink their works to tameness, those of Douw have a vigour and an expression never excelled by any artist of his age. His pictures of Dutch life are perfect. "The Village School," in the Museum of Amsterdam, is often quoted for its peculiar power, and the difficulty the artist created for himself only to conquer it.

Fig. 103.—Leyden.

It represents a large room filled with figures, and lighted by four candles at different parts of the composition. But a finer, if not the finest work by Douw, is the picture in the Louvre, known as "La Femme Hydropique," which displays his wonderful colour, drawing, composition, and knowledge of effect, in the most satisfactory manner.

In Gerard Douw's works we view the superior life of the
Dutch. He has no love for the delineation of vulgar or coarse
scenes, such as delighted too many of his compeers, and gave too
much weight to critical objections to their works in general.
Refined minds, used to the purities and high resolves of the
Italian schools, received a repulsive shock from the scenes of
Brauwer and Jan Steen, and could scarcely tolerate the simple
truth of Teniers, or the grand imaginings of Rubens, accompanied by the coarseness which seemed almost inseparable from
the governing ideas of these masters. Ostade, on the contrary,
elevates all he touches; his youthful figures breathe health and
win affection; his men and women are not the tanned and
wrinkled creatures repulsive to eye and mind, but rather lovable
from the deeply-traced furrows with which sixty winters of genial
thought have seamed their faces—"frosty" the end of their
life scarcely seems, it is so "kindly" withal; and if we would
pleasantly dream over the old time in Holland, and live in
imagination among the people of the seventeenth century, we
must go to the works of Ostade and Douw (Fig. 104).

It is by studying the paintings of Jan Steen we become most
intimately acquainted with the everyday life of the Dutch. Like
our own Hogarth, he had the keenest sense of humour; and, like
him, he has been too frequently stigmatised as a slovenly painter,
or as a caricaturist. Both artists handled their pencils freely
enough, but they only did as much by one touch as less
impressible minds could do by a dozen; while their equally
powerful perception of humorous character led them to fix its

broadest features on their canvas. Careful execution, free conception, vivid and powerful colour, and vigorous *chiaro-oscuro*,
are declared by Dr. Waagen to be found in the works of Jan

Fig. 104.—Hall of an Old House, Leyden.

Steen. Dr. Kügler says, "They imply a clear and cheerful view
of common life, treated with a careless humour, and accompanied
by great force and variety of individual expression, such as

evinces the sharpest observation. He is almost the only artist of the Netherlands who has thus, with true genius, brought into full play all those elements of comedy. His technical execution suits his design; it is carefully finished, and, notwithstanding the closest attention to minute details, is as firm and correct as it is free and light." In the landscape backgrounds of some of his pictures—such as "The Game of Skittles," in Lord Ashburton's gallery—we find qualities which the late J. M. W. Turner declared "worthy of Cuyp." Some of his scenes of better-class life—such as that known as "The Parrot," in the gallery at Amsterdam—are full of grace and careful manipulation. It is, however, chiefly by such pictures as his "Feast of St. Nicholas," in the same collection, that he is best known; here his humour and expression are so great, that a French critic says you seem to know the thoughts of each person in the picture. In Mr. Baring's gallery there is a marvellous instance of his power— an old woman looking up with a grotesque earnestness into a doctor's face, who has come to attend her daughter. The lifelike energy and vivid expression of fleeting humour in each feature are perfectly wonderful. It is at once simply and boldly painted, as if the expression had been caught by photography.

As reckless as Brauwer, Steen lived a happier life: he was idle, gay, and thoughtless, but not vicious. Always poor, and careless of money when he had it, he rattled through life, taking its rough lessons with perfect good humour, and never caring for the morrow. He was born at Leyden, in 1636, and died there in 1689. He married early, and had several children. His wife, like himself, was careless and equally improvident; she appears to have been quite as neglectful of all household duties and provisions for the future as her husband. If what is affirmed of some of his paintings be true, they represent her in no creditable state of ebriety, and her whole household in confusion. Unluckily, they both started in life in a brewery at Delft, which was furnished for them by the artist's father, who was in that trade. The young couple, however, kept their taps constantly running for their own use and that of their friends, until bankruptcy closed the doors, and Steen took up art for a fresh living. The life of a tavern-keeper had, however, too great a charm for Jan to relinquish readily, and he came back to Leyden on the death of his father, and opened house as one of that fraternity. Hither soon came all the topers of the town, and many a careless artist to boot. Among them were Mieris and Lievens; the figure of Peace extending her olive branch, which Jan painted for his sign, was indicative of the little trouble the painter-publican chose to give his customers. Hence the topers never troubled themselves to pay, and Jan, faithful to his sign, gave them no uneasiness about it, until again compelled to close his too friendly doors through debt. His careless wife died soon after; and his neglected children frequently became the models for many of his pictures. He contracted a second marriage with a woman who sold sheep's heads and "trotters" in the butcher's market; and he painted, and drank, and took the world easy until his death, when he left his wife with nine children, one of whom took to sculpture as a profession.

In spite of his culpable carelessness, and love of slatternly
ease and tap-room life, he had superior friends. The gentlemanly
Karel du Moor painted his humble second wife's portrait to
gratify them both; Gabriel Metzu, the quiet and elegant
delineator of Dutch aristocratic life, was also his friend, and
sat with his wife to Jan for their portraits; and Mieris, we have
already noted, was his boon-companion. The elegance of the
pictures by this latter artist, who always chose the higher life of
Holland, like his fellow-artist, Metzu, for the subjects of his
pencil, and delineated such scenes so admirably, would scarcely
have led to the conclusion that he could have found pleasure
in Jan's tavern at Leyden. But the fact is that Jan was a sound
artist, and could mix up agreeable knowledge with his farcical
jovialities. The orgies of Jan's tavern proved so fascinating,
that it is recorded Mieris was nearly drowned one night in a
dyke as he returned home in one of what Burns calls "The
wee short hours ayont the twal," rather the worse for liquor.
The painter was fished out by a cobbler, who, astonished at
his velvet dress and gold buttons, was still more surprised to find
the saved man only a poor painter; but most astonished of
all when the artist, in his gratitude, made him a present of one of
his pictures, for which he obtained eight hundred florins.

It is in the works of Jan Steen that we more particularly
see the ordinary life of the Dutch people depicted. Their
manners and customs may be there truly studied. "The Feast
of St. Nicholas," at the museum at Amsterdam, and "The Marriage," in the collection of Mr. Baring, illustrate our meaning.

Stolid and unchanging as Dutchmen appear to be, two centuries have not passed over their country without producing very considerable changes in it. While the tourist will note, as we have already done, much that reminds him of his first impressions of Dutch life obtained from Dutch pictures, there is also much that has passed away from the land for ever, and which only exists in such representations. You still observe the ivy-grown farm-house, with its "thick-pleached orchard," and its quaint walls and gates; but you see no longer the loosely-dressed boor, with his wide Spanish doublet and balloon-breeches. Paris has invaded Holland, and the *Magazin des Modes* has had power enough to transform a Dutchman into a comparatively fashionable being. Village life now is not the village life of Ostade and Gerard Douw—it is less picturesque and less slatternly; it displays more of Dutch formality than we see in their works, but it has more of comfort and respectability. It is in the quiet village inns that are still scattered over the land we may now detect the last relics of old manners. As you approach the principal towns you see many of these welcome hostelries, the doors bowered over with grape vines, and looking worthy the pencil of an Ostade, while the long shed beside their trim gardens may, mentally, be easily peopled by the skittle and tric-trac players of Teniers. In the open space before the house a tall pole, some thirty feet in height, is frequently to be observed; it is crowned on gala days with a sort of weathercock, and the wooden bars, placed at some distance around it, are the marks where the men stand to shoot at it. It is the old *papeguay*, or fictitious parrot, which exercised the ability of the young villagers at a time when archery was generally enforced as a practice. In our country the custom was also adopted, and shooting at the popinjay was as usual in an English village of the time of Elizabeth as it was among the Dutch, who still preserve their village life more unchanged than we do. Popular customs are at all times the last to succumb to fashion; and while large towns vary continually, and take the most recent tone of manners, the village goes on in the present generation pretty much as it did in the last. Novelties are not so welcome there, and are looked upon generally with a characteristic distrust.

But while we speak of changes in Holland since the days of the old painters who have made its past age famous, it must be borne in mind that they are the slow results of nearly two centuries, and after all by no means make so great a change during that long period as has been effected elsewhere. Even in the towns many old customs are retained that have been in use time-out-of-mind, and which have been immortalised in some picture of one or other of the old masters of Holland. We have already noted the humorous works of Jan Steen as the truest transcripts of the manners which he saw around him. One of them depicts a fellow dancing joyously into a room with a fresh herring in his hand, exultingly upheld by the tail. His antics are received with a broad smile from all present. It would be difficult for an ordinary spectator to understand all this, did he not know that a fresh herring is considered by the Dutch a panacea for every complaint; and their arrival on their shores is hailed with so much joy, that the first who hears the news generally makes it publicly known by hanging at his door a frame, decorated with evergreen flowers and coloured paper, in honour of the joyful event (Fig. 105). This silent mode of communicating intelligence is used on other occasions. Thus, at Haarlem, it is a custom on the birth of a child to affix to the principal door, to denote the event, a pincushion, which

Fig. 105.—The Herring Sign.

is constructed of red silk, covered with lace, and deeply fringed. The sex of the child is defined by a small piece of white paper placed between the lace and cushion if it is a girl, but the absence of all mark denotes a boy (Fig. 106). This custom has other and solid advantages; it not only prevents intrusive curiosity, but for a certain period the house is protected from actions for debt—no bailiffs dare molest it, no soldiers can be billeted on it, and when troops march past the drums invariably cease to beat.*

One Dutch town is so much like another that but for a few remnants of an ancient kind they would become monotonous to the stranger. Some of these relics are extremely picturesque; and at Haarlem the old Butchery is so costly and beautiful a building, with its varied walls of white stone and red brick, and

its richly-carved decorations, as to make it one of the principal features of the town. We must, however, go back to old engravings if we would see the very streets in which the men of the days of Douw and Mieris walked. Fortunately, their features have been preserved in old engravings scattered through books sometimes devoted to subjects of another kind. Our view of the stadtholder's house at Haarlem (Fig. 107), and the surrounding buildings, is of this nature; and is copied from La Serre's very curious volume

Fig. 106.—The Birth-Token.

descriptive of the reception given to the queen-mother, Queen Catherine de Medici, by the principal Dutch towns, in the year 1635, when she paid a visit to the Low Countries on her way to her daughter Henrietta-Maria, the queen of Charles I., performing

---

* The custom is traditionally reported to have originated owing to the death of a merchant's wife, whose house had been entered noisily and rudely by officers, on the occasion of his bankruptcy, during her confinement.

the journey from Bar-le-Duc to Gorcum, and crossing the sea from thence to Harwich.

Some of the Dutch towns are less altered in their general features than might have been imagined, and this is strikingly the case with the chief of them, Amsterdam. The peculiar nature

Fig. 107.—The Stadtholder's House, Haarlem, 1635.

of its foundations, and the difficulty of tampering with its necessary arrangements, may have induced this. The visitor at the present time looking at it across from Waterland, will see a city in no degree changed in its broad aspect from the days of Rembrandt. When Catherine de Medici made her "happy entry" into that city, in 1635, its features from this point were delineated by De Vlieger, and have been copied in our cut (Fig. 108). It might have been sketched yesterday, so completely does it give the striking characteristics of this old city of the sea.

The Hague, as it appeared during the palmy era of Dutch art, is seen in another of our cuts, and that being the "fashionable" locality has changed most; indeed, there has been a

Fig. 108.—Amsterdam, 1635.

visible desire to make it accord to the refinements and tastes of modern high life, as much as can be consistent with national character (Fig. 109). It is the residence of the court, and is to Amsterdam what the Versailles of the days of Louis XIV. was to Paris. There is one characteristic feature of the Hague which has remained unchanged,—and that is the favourite promenade on the road to Scheveningen, or Scheveling, as it is sometimes called. It is an avenue of oaks and limes, nearly three miles in length, perfectly straight, and bounded by the little steeple of the parish church of Scheveningen at the farther end, which may be seen from the Hague. The trees are here allowed to grow in full luxuriance, and shadow the road, which is never lonely—for the Hague is the most pleasant and healthy

Fig. 109.—The Hague, 1635.

of Dutch towns, and the favourite resort of the Hollander. The refreshing sea-breeze may always be inhaled here; hence pedestrians and equestrians choose this road, and the idle find constant amusement in sitting under the trees and watching the passers-by. Scheveningen is a little fishing village on the sea-shore, occupied by about three hundred fishermen, and

C C

their carts may be met on this road in the morning, drawn by
strong dogs, conveying fish to the Hague (Fig. 110). The situation
of the village itself is particularly dreary; the sea-margin is a
sandy desert, planted here and there with rushes to prevent

Fig. 110.—The Road to Scheveningen.

the sand from blowing over-land in stormy weather. It is of
interest in English history as the place from whence King
Charles II. embarked to resume the sovereignty of England,* and
as the birth-place of William III.

---

* There is a very interesting and curious picture, representing this event with true Dutch
minuteness, in the Gallery at Hampton Court.

The pictures of Metzu, Mieris, and Terburg exhibit the
highest tone of Dutch society,—the wealth and comfort of their
indoor life, the richness of their apparel, the simple dignity
of their bearing. A Dutchman may feel proud of the ancestry
delineated by his native painters, of the patriots who fought and
bled more determinedly for their liberties than the men of any
other nation have been called upon to do. In the really grand
picture at Amsterdam, representing the city-guard met to
celebrate the important treaty of Münster, which gave independence to the Dutch after long years of Spanish treachery and
cruelty, the painter has truthfully portrayed men, certainly
without ideal gracefulness, but with innate manly dignity which
gives a lifelike charm to the picture, and has obtained for
Van der Helst the highest position in this branch of art.* To a
morally-balanced mind the home-scenes of such painters are
as capable of imparting pleasure as the more ambitious attempts
of the heroic school, inasmuch as they generally steer clear of
anachronisms and false sentiment. Art is catholic in its views,
and should be received on broad principles; it would be unfair to
disregard a Greek cameo because it does not overpower the

---

* Sir Joshua Reynolds has given his opinion of this noble picture in the strongest
manner; he says it is " perhaps the finest picture of portraits in the world, comprehending
more of those qualities which make a perfect portrait than any other I have ever seen."
Kügler also testifies to its truth, boldness, and brilliancy. It has been recently very
carefully and beautifully engraved, but we lose in the engraving the admirable colouring
which gives so great a charm to the noble original, making it rival in attractiveness the
" Night Guard " of Rembrandt, which hangs opposite to it in the Gallery of the Hague.
Two such pictures may be sought in vain elsewhere.

eye like a bas-relief by Phidias—particularly as a study of both would assure us that the same great principles governed the mind which produced each. The minute finish which some find objectionable in such works as those of Douw and Ostade, may be excused as necessary results from minds schooled to patient labour, but they never forgot the true fundamental principles of art; for however laboured their works appear, their design and general arrangement of colour are broad and bold. As compositions they may be viewed at any distance satisfactorily, but they will also reward the nearest scrutiny.

The painters just named were particularly happy in the delineation of what are sometimes termed "conversation-pieces"—an old-fashioned designation which is singularly and usefully characteristic of such designs. In them we see a sort of photographed view of old Dutch manners. The wealth of Holland peeps forth in every one of them. The costly silks, velvets, and furs of the ladies, are rivalled by the velvets, feathers, and gold lace of their gallants. The ebony cabinets, carved chairs, and massive furniture, which generally fill the rooms delineated, display the wealth and love of comfort which reigned paramount in the dwellings of the rich merchants of the Low Countries. The very ponderosity of the various articles are characteristic; so also are the Indian jars and carpets, the parrots and monkeys, which hint very plainly the far-sighted spirit of trading enterprise that gave the Dutch nation a well-deserved pre-eminence in the seventeenth century. The traveller may yet trace in Holland the old love for the products of Eastern taste and skill, and the porcelain of China and Japan is still the ordinary ware of the Dutchman; he also revels in a Chinese summer-house, and delights in a monkey or an aviary of birds, whose notes seem but the outpourings of a sad reminiscence of a sunny land far away, to which they will never return.

Imitative art can never be carried further than it was by Terburg in his famous picture known as "The Satin Gown," a picture which has been made more known by the notice it has received by Goethe in his "Wahlverwandschaften." He describes it as representing a noble, knightly-looking man, who sits with one leg over the other addressing himself to the conscience of his daughter, who stands before him. "She is a majestic figure, in a full and flowing dress of white satin; her back only is seen, but the whole attitude shows that she is struggling with her feelings. The mother, too, seems to be concealing a little embarrassment, for she looks into a wine-glass out of which she is sipping." The extraordinary qualities it possesses as a transcript of Nature are unrivalled, and the satin gown of the principal figure is reality itself.

There was a still lower class of imitative art practised with unremitting patience and assiduity by some few Dutch painters. They devoted themselves to "still-life," and produced representations of the humblest furniture of the kitchen. At the head of this class stands William Kalf, who was born at Amsterdam in 1630, and died in 1693, having devoted his life not only to the delineations of the gold and silver cups* of the wealthy burgomaster, but to the humblest utilities of his establishment. Yet such simple subjects give the painter opportunities for composition, colour, and *chiaro-oscuro* of the finest kind. He brought great rules of art to bear on all he delineated, and he elevated the commonplace to the poetic. "In the treatment even of these things there is an ideal, or beautiful, as distinct from a literal imitation."†

The camp life of the Dutch was ably represented by a series of painters, who delighted to depict

"Battle's magnificently stern array."

It was, unhappily, too common a sight in Holland; the history of the country is that of one continuous struggle for freedom. The frightful scenes which Callot has depicted in his "Miseries of War" were enacted over and over again by the cruel agents of the Duke of Alva upon the devoted and suffering people. While they must have hated the sight of a Spanish trooper, they must have looked with joy on the native defenders of their country. Certainly, never were soldiers braver than the soldiers of Holland; never did men fight more devotedly for a country; never were imperishable deeds of pure patriotism graven deeper

---

* The Dutch poet who composed his epitaph declares in it, that all the plate he ever painted would not be sufficient reward to so virtuous a man as was the refined and patient painter of these metallic treasures, many of which are remarkable for their fancy and taste in design.

† Leslie, "Lectures on Painting," p. 243.

on the eternal tablets of fame. We see only in the painting of the Hollander the picturesque features of war—

> " The mounting in hot haste the steed,
>   The mustering squadron and the clattering car,
>   That pouring forward with impetuous speed
>   Doth swiftly form the solid ranks of war."

The prince of painters in this branch of art is Philip Wouvermans. There is a picturesque beauty given by him to camp-life, which has an irresistible charm for the eye. We see the bustle which follows the trumpeter's call to horse; we notice the readiness of the well-caparisoned officer, the grudging departure of the common soldier, absorbed in gambling or drinking till the last moment has arrived to fall into the ranks. The gaiety of the uniforms, the beauty and vigour of the horses, the entire "pictorial element" which reigns over the scene, makes us feel that war thus

> " Hid in magnificence, and drowned in state,
>   Loses the fiend."

It is a proof that the world has increased in humanity as the last two centuries have passed over it; for it has been the province of modern art alone to rob war of its false glories, and teach us to look on the reverse of the picture. Never was a poem more touchingly written than that which Sir Edwin Landseer has painted in his pictures of "Peace" and "War:" never did philosopher descant more convincingly on the text that it is chiefly

> " Man's inhumanity to man
> Makes countless thousands mourn."

Wouvermans was the perfect type of a Dutchman—reserved, industrious, and eminently fond of home. During his whole lifetime he lived in Haarlem (Fig. 111), unvarying the calm tenour of his course. From such a reserved man one would hardly expect these vivid pictures of peculiar phases of life. He also

Fig. 111.—Gate at Haarlem.

delighted in painting jovial parties of sportsmen—sometimes riding out with ladies, equipped for hawking, and sometimes galloping over heath and plain after the hunted stag, or reposing in the cool shade near a spring. Kügler, who notes this, also remarks, that "one of the points of interest in these pictures

is the feeling for well-bred society and decorum, assisted by some
little hint at a novel-like relation between the personages
represented. The other main point of interest in Wouverman's

Fig. 112.—Wouvermans.

pictures is derived from the taste and knowledge with which
he delighted to paint the horse, that constant companion of
the out-door-life of a gentleman, in all its various and manifold

D D

situations. In many of his works the horse is treated as the
principal figure; he painted him in the stable, being saddled,
in the *manége*, when taken to water or to the fair (Fig. 113).
Other subjects which afford opportunity for prominently displaying the figure of the horse—such as battles, attacks by
robbers, or adventures of carriers—were frequently painted by

Fig. 113.

him." He had a somewhat ideal mode of treating landscape
accessories, which are all subservient to the general effect of the
figures introduced. Although his brother Peter was one of the
most successful imitators of his peculiarities, Philip may be
safely said to have originated and upheld by his own genius
a peculiar phase of art, which has never since been so successfully cultivated.

Van der Meulen, more ambitious, and less caring for the quietude of home-life, became a camp-follower of Louis XIV., and painted the campaigns of that monarch from observation, industriously covering the walls of Versailles with pictures of its master's heroism ; and here the *Grande Monarque* could repose amid the contemplation of his own glories, and listen to the adulations of Boileau and Racine. The full-dressed glories of his battles, as depicted by his Dutch servant, seem to render war a mere showy masquerade, did we not see the devastation which proceeds far away from king and courtier in the distance, and know from the truer page of history the wanton and wicked invasions this cold-hearted voluptuary continually made upon better men than himself.

Marine-painting more naturally fell within the scope of the Hollander, and nowhere else did the art flourish so well as among the Dutch painters. Ludolf Backhuysen and William Van der Velde are names which take highest place in this department. It is recorded that Admiral de Ruyter ordered cannon to be fired from his noble vessels of war, for the express purpose of its effects being studied by the latter artist when engaged in painting his sea-fights.

It therefore is in "the actual," as exhibited in every phase of life and nature, that the artists of Holland achieved their position ; but paramount as their claims may be in this particular, we find sublimity combined with it in the works of Rembrandt, and poetry in Cuyp and Ruysdael. All is, however, strongly tinged with native feeling, so unmistakably pronounced that we could not mistake a Dutch picture for the production of the painters of any other nation. It is as visible in the landscapes of Hobbema as it is in the peasant scenes of Ostade. But it was chiefly the popular scenes of Dutch life by the genre-painters that gave celebrity to this new school of art, and made it generally popular.

We by no means intend in this place to combat the objections made to this style of art by the admirers of the ideal school, or the elevated conceptions of the great masters of Italy; but simply to plead for the fact of as much ideality and poetry existing in the works of the Dutch as their sphere of action will allow. We plead for their truth; for the perfect art-power they have in displaying this truth; for the sentiment and feeling that continually lurk beneath it, to gratify all who will diligently search for it, there as elsewhere in the world it remains—hidden from merely superficial observation. M. Charles Blanc has grappled with the most difficult portion of this subject when treating of the works of Rembrandt; we will only, therefore, refer to the labours of such artists among the other painters of the Low Countries as make ordinary life the subjects of their pencils. Leslie, in his "Lectures," has put these claims clearly. He says, "The great merit of the Flemish and Dutch painters is the absence of all affected and mawkish sensibility—all that stage trickery on the spectator, by which he is made to believe himself touched to the heart. This false sentiment began with Greuze, and has ever since more or less infected art." Their power of conveying interest to the most ordinary actions he illustrates by one public example. He says, "There are few pictures in our National Gallery before which I find myself more often standing than the very small one by Maas, the subject of which is the scraping of a parsnip. A decent-looking Dutch housewife sits intently engaged in this operation, with a fine chubby child standing by her side watching the process, as children will stand and watch the most ordinary operations, with an intensity of interest as if the very existence of the whole world depended on the exact manner in which that parsnip was scraped. It is not the colour and light and shadow of this charming little gem, superlative as they are, that constitute its great attraction ; for a mere outline of it would arrest attention among a thousand subjects of its class, and many pictures as beautiful in effect might not interest so much ; but it is the delight at seeing a trait of childhood we have often observed and been amused with in Nature, for the first time so felicitously given by art. I have noticed the natural manner in which Raphael and other great painters represented children as wholly uninterested in that which engages the attention of their elders. Here the incident is exactly the reverse, and treated with equal felicity." It may startle some few minds to find this conjunction of the names of Raphael and Maas ; but no happier instance could prove the fact that

> "One touch of Nature makes the whole world kin."

If we owe the artists of Holland no other gratitude for their labours, let us at least award them this their just due—all honour for the true and persevering study of Nature. The world had been in danger of losing simplicity in art, and getting the laboured results of scholastic rules instead : an art that every one might comprehend, and be improved by the comprehension, was evolved from the ateliers of Holland. It taught that the world around us is filled with poetry to reward the ardent seeker of the beautiful, and it displayed this truth with all the vigour of an honest nature.

The lives of these artists are instructive even in their unobtrusiveness. Brief as our notices have necessarily been of their career, there is little more to record of them. They passed their lives in the closest study of Nature, and found in her varied beauties enough to employ it well in imitating her charms ; content in the sphere of action to which their genius had assigned them, they worked on regardless of the more prosaic men around them, and patiently waited the recognition of the inherent truth of their works. Some were honoured in their own day, and reaped the harvest they had sown, but others lived poor and died neglected ; yet who shall say they were not happier men than the wealthier merchants of their land? Untrammelled by the cares of trade, and freely roaming in scenes his heart responds to, the painter, however poor, is wealthy in his nobler aspirations after the beautiful, implanted in the world by the divine hand of its Maker. The mammon-worshipping professor of art may be endued with genius occasionally, but he is a *rara avis*, and is considerably outnumbered by his less wealthy brethren. It is, however, essential to greatness that it be allied to devotion, and that cannot be without some abandonment of self. The world, it has been said, frequently knows nothing of its greatest men; but are not such men made great by abstraction from its narrowing jealousies, its struggles for power, its sacrifice of simplicity and pure-mindedness at the shrine of wealth and worldliness?

THE DUTCH LANDSCAPE AND FLOWER-PAINTERS.

THE DUTCH LANDSCAPE AND FLOWER-PAINTERS.

LANDSCAPE-PAINTING as an independent art, is the youngest of the category. Beautiful as were the background views introduced into the works of the old painters, they were backgrounds merely, and secondary to the main intention of the picture. As an art self-reliant in its claims, it does not appear to have come boldly forth, willing to stand on its own merits, before the close of the sixteenth century. It is to the artists of the Low Countries that we owe this now popular branch of art. The landscape backgrounds of the early German and Flemish masters certainly originated the art, but it was the later painters of Holland who perfected its power. Appended to Kügler's remarks, in his "Handbook of Painting," that "Landscape, in the hands of Titian and Giorgione, sometimes assumed an independent character, and it is said that Titian was the first to treat it as a separate branch of Art," we have this note, by Sir Charles Eastlake—"Landscape-painting in Italy, however independent in its perfection, appears in its origin to have been indebted, in more than one instance, to a German influence. Vasari distinctly says that Titian kept some German landscape-painters in his house, and studied with them for some months. In Bologna it is probable that Denys Calvert, a Flemish artist, first excited the emulation of the Caracci, Domenichino, and others, who, in the end, formed so distinguished a school of landscape-painters. In both these instances a certain resemblance to the German manner, however differently modified by the character of the schools, is to be recognised, especially in the umbellated treatment of the foliage." It is impossible for any student of mediæval art not to have been frequently struck by the great beauty of the landscape backgrounds introduced into the historic or religious pictures of that period. It is true that they are always conventionally treated, and rendered subservient to the ruling *motive* of the picture ; but we cannot wonder that landscape should eventually assert its own sole power of charming, by the repose and beauty it imparts, even when used as a simple accessory. The works of Van Eyck, Memling, and Dürer, frequently allow landscape to share at least one half of the attention of the spectator ; and they appear to have intended this, to give a certain *air* to their compositions which would else be wanting. It was their avowed object to delineate great space, and they did this by invariably carrying the eye of the spectator to the extreme distance of the view by concentrating the light upon the horizon : nothing can exceed the brilliancy, beauty, clearness, and depth of space exhibited in these early works. It induced others of the school to go further, and make the figures in a historical or religious picture secondary to it ; but it was not until the beginning of the seventeenth century that the grand conceptions of Poussin and Rubens gave entire independence to this branch of art, and proved its innate power to command alone its own tribe of worshippers. The Dutch painters afterwards persevered in the new track until the triumph was complete.

The fantastic redundancy of details, the conventional forms of trees, and the equally conventional treatment of the general effect in very early landscapes by the artists of the Low Countries, were completely cast aside in the grander and truer works which resulted from the *atelier* of Holland. Annibale Caracci had sometimes devoted himself to the delineation of the scenery of the Apennines; and contemporary with him there lived at Rome Paul Bril, who, born at Antwerp, combined the taste of his native school with that of the greater Italian. Suddenly, a series of landscape-painters appear upon the stage, and the early parts of the century saw the master-minds of Poussin and Rubens joined by Claude, the most charming of all. He received his early training from the Fleming, Paul Bril; and one great trait of the early school is visible in his works—the love of repose, and the idea of air and space, given by condensing the light on the horizon, or in the extreme distance of the picture. The ideal beauty thus evolved in the works of these great men kept up and stimulated the school of landscape-painters in the Low Countries, and contemporary with Claude and John Both, were Jacob Ruysdael, John Wynants, John Baptist Weenix, and his greater pupil, Nicholas Berghem, who were all occupied on landscape solely; while such master-minds as those of Cuyp and Potter made its beauties an integral part of their immortal works. Rembrandt had devoted his powerful genius to the display of effects hitherto undeveloped in the art, and the grandeur with which he invested a simple landscape by the aid of powerful *chiaro-oscuro,* and the study of storm and sunshine, as in his famous " Three Trees," vindicated the art from a low level, and gave it a position that only the genius of our own great masters, Gainsborough, Constable, Wilson, Turner, Linnell, and others, could elevate.

This youngest daughter of the arts, though unquestionably the favourite of the public, has been received by her sisters in some degree as an interloper, and her claim to equal sympathy denied.   Surely this is unjust: is God's beautiful world less to be valued, or less worthy our study, than the world of man's passion? " Rocks, trees, mountains, plains, and waters," says Leslie, " are the features of landscape; but its expression is from above.   The love of landscape is a love so pure that it can never associate with the relishes of a mere voluptuary, and wherever such a love is native, it is the certain indication of a superior mind."   Constable declared of one of Gainsborough's landscapes, " I cannot think of it, even now, without tears in my eyes."   How many of Constable's pictures are redolent of all the freshness of earth's beauties! so fresh, so pure, that we may almost exclaim with Gray—

> " I feel the gales that from ye blow
> A momentary bliss bestow."

Any eulogy on Turner, whose pictures are poems, would be inappropriate here; an abler pen has enforced his claims to honour. We would merely remark that it is unbecoming in Englishmen, at any rate, to depreciate this lovely art; for, rivalled as we may be in other branches, in this the genius of English painters is acknowledged to be supreme.

In the pictures by Ruysdael there is a grandeur of composition and a boldness of treatment which belong to no other Dutch landscape-painter. He alone displays mountain scenery and foaming cataracts, which must have been idealisations in a great degree—he could not have studied the grand features he depicts in the monotony of his own land, which some authors assure us he never quitted. It has been conjectured that he rambled to Guelderland and Westphalia; but, allowing this, he must have exaggerated what he could see there, to produce the noble mountains and boldly-dashing waterfalls he delighted to depict.* He was born at Haarlem in 1636 (Fig. 115), and was the son of a picture-frame maker. Of a gloomy and reserved temper, he lived alone, and died poor in 1681; yet his works have a rare

---

* It has been asserted that Ruysdael constructed models to paint from, composed of small twigs and fractured stones, which he exaggerated into trees and mountains, and so composed his works. Such antagonisms might be doubted, had we not other instances where the artistic mind has been stimulated by the very opposite means that would ordinarily be supposed were used. Thus it is known of Guido that his most beautiful female heads were painted from a male colour-grinder, who is described as perfectly hideous, and whose features were transformed into a Magdalen, with the same *pose* and *chiaro-oscuro*, but with perfect beauty; the artist evidently using his model as a means of producing beauty by contrast alone.

excellence. The ideality which invests his scenes is gloomily

grand, worthy of the solitary man who lived only for his art, and saw only the severe or terrible features of nature. If he

painted a native scene, which seldom occurred, it is invested with
the mournful gloom of Holland, rather than with the happier
features depicted by other artists. His pictures are to landscape-
art what the Spanish school is to the French—vigorous and
grand, but terrible. His scholars, Hobbema and De Vries, lose

Fig. 115.—Street in Haarlem.

his gloom ; but the former retains much of his grandeur, though
devoted to less ambitious scenes.

Casting away all lugubrious views of his own country,
Berghem delighted in representing simple nature in full joyous-
ness. In this quality he differs from most masters of the Dutch

F F

school. He is the very reverse of his friend Ruysdael. The gloomy grandeur of his solitary and poetic mind impresses itself on the scenes he depicts; and you cannot study them without a feeling of "divine melancholy" creeping over the mind. Berghem, on the contrary, delights in bright skies, light clouds, and cheerful pastoral scenes. Unlike Ruysdael, he seeks not northern gloom, but rather southern sunshine. He was born at Haarlem in 1624, and was the son of Peter Van Haerlem,* a painter of very moderate ability, who lived by delineating those pictures of still-life in which the Hollanders delighted. He had, however, excellent instruction from the artists who knew his father, and who liked the cheerful disposition of the son; and his uncle Weenix, whose daughter he married, improved his tastes. He was intimate in the best part of his life with Wouvermans, Everdingen, Both, and Ruysdael; and his time passed happily in the varied society of such friends. With them, or with nature, or else in delineating her better features in his own studio, he knew peace; but not with his wife, who was in disposition sordid, while the painter possessed the geniality of soul which beams forth on his canvas. It is related of her that she constantly spurred him to exertion by knocking against the wall of his studio, and kept his earnings that he might not

---

* The name he is popularly known by is a *sobriquet*, which originated, it is said, in his escaping from the infliction of some chastisement from his father's house to that of the painter Van Goyen, who, fearful that the irritated parent should reach him, called to the inmates, *Berg hem* (or, hide him).

indulge his taste for old prints. In the Château of Bentheim, where he resided, he had but to walk to the windows of his studio to gaze on green meadows, luxuriant trees, and cattle in every variety of grouping. Some writers affirm that he must have travelled to Italy, and could not have obtained by the aid of his own large collection of prints the ruins and temples he so well depicted in some of his works. They do not, however, sufficiently take into consideration the great constructiveness of some artistic minds—the way they comprehend one object through another. All Berghem's southern scenes are really translated into Dutch. His power of imitation is known to have been so great, that he could deceive connoisseurs by painting in the precise style of other artists.

He had many pupils, among whom the only happy hours of his life passed. Karel Dujardin is conjectured to have been one; but he certainly taught Peter de Hooge, Dirk Maas, and Artus Van der Neer. This latter artist delighted to paint the effects of evening and night. "A piece of water in a wood, surrounded by high dark trees; a lonely canal, whose tranquil surface reflects the light of the moon; a city in repose, steeped in the quiet moonlight—sometimes the calm peacefulness of night broken by the glaring light of a conflagration; these are the subjects which Van der Neer delighted to repeat in the most free and pleasing style; and with these he again and again rivets the eyes of the spectators."* In our National Gallery we possess a

---

* Kügler's "Handbook of Painting."

charming specimen of his power of conveying the peculiar effects of moonlight—an effect which could not be secured by sketching, and therefore argues a most retentive memory for the varied hues of nature.

There is another and a distinct class of students of nature whom the Dutch school originated—they who "represent what may be called the still-life of field-plants, under whose friendly shelter beetles and lizards, little birds and snakes, pass their unheeded existence;"* or who depict the magnificent bouquets in richly-sculptured vases, with which the rich merchant princes of Holland decorated their mansions; or else dispose of them in "most admired disorder, strewn upon a table, or entwined around a picture or bas-relief." John Breughel was one of the earliest artists who delighted in making pictures of these "stars of the earth;" and he was succeeded and outstripped by his scholar, Daniel Seghers, who first grouped their forms and colours into harmonious conjunction, and carried high principles of composition into his works. A peculiar poetic feeling also pervades the flower-painting of John David de Heem; and from his *atelier* proceeded many excellent scholars, and among them some few ladies, to whom the art has always presented charms. The most celebrated lady flower-painter was Rachel Ruysch, or Van Pool, her married name, who flourished in the latter half of the seventeenth and beginning of the eighteenth

---

* Kügler's "Handbook of Painting."

century. At the same period lived John Van Huysum, whose flowers are said to want only perfume to make them real.

This celebrated artist was born at Amsterdam in 1682, and was the son of a house-decorator. The incidents of his life consist, as usual with Dutch artists, of the catalogue of his works. Between painting at home and visiting the flower-gardens of Haarlem, his days passed quietly away. He died in 1749, after having enjoyed great patronage for his works, which were sold at a high rate, and were sought for by most of the European sovereigns and nobles.

The taste for decorative gardening and rare flowers was at this period carried to the greatest extent; men would ruin themselves to possess a certain tulip-bulb; the records of no country produce parallels to the mania for flowers which once beset the Hollander. Haarlem was the grand centre of their growth, and thither came rich amateurs from all parts of Holland, as well as from distant countries.* The flower-gardens of this city are still famous, and hyacinth-bulbs are even now sent from thence to all parts of Europe. One of Captain Cook's companions declared that when at sea, opposite the coast beyond Haarlem, when the wind set from the land, "through the placid atmosphere we could distinguish the balsamic odour of the hyacinth and other flowers?"

---

* It is recorded that the anemone was first brought to England from a Dutch garden, whose proprietor was so chary of his flowers that on no consideration would he part with plant or seed. The visitor accordingly arrayed himself in a shaggy great coat, which brushed the seed from the plant in passing, and which was carefully gathered from the folds of the garment after his departure from the garden.

There can be no more beautiful sight than these Dutch gardens, with their glorious beds of flowers. The soil of Holland seems to suit their growth, and the brightness of their hues contrasts forcibly with the deep green of the trees and hedges. Wherever you travel in this country you see this love of pleasure-gardens ; and over the decoration and "stock" large sums of money are expended. Rows of summer-houses gay with the brightest colours line the canals, each inscribed with a name or motto, as "Rosenthal," "Lilienthal," &c., or "Lust en rust" (Pleasure and ease), "Niet zoo zwaalyk" (Not so bad!) "Vriendschap en gezelschap" (Friendship and sociality), "Het vermaak is in't hovenieren" (There is pleasure in gardening), &c. Here the men smoke and the ladies knit, amusing themselves with looking out on the passers-by. In front of its windows a canal or ditch stagnates, its waters only disturbed by the passage of a boat, or the plash of the enormous water-rats or frogs with which they abound. Thus, in the words of Beckford, "Every flower that wealth can purchase diffuses its perfume on one side ; while every stench a canal can exhale poisons the air on the other." The gardens of the ancient châteaux of Holland were much more artistic than the modern : arcades were formed of clipped yews, or trained creepers, over trellisses supported by caryatides, as shown in our cut from a Dutch print dated 1653 (Fig. 116). Now they are generally quite square, bounded by clipped hedges, with every walk geometrically true, and embellished with rows of stiff poplars, or square-cut trees at each angle, to complete the monotony ; a fish-pond generally occupies the centre ; or, if the garden be a small one, a small post is placed in the midst, supporting a large glass globe darkened inside, and which serves as a mirror to reflect the neighbourhood all around it.   Trim box borders edge each parterre, which is religiously devoted to the display of one kind of flower alone, and nothing like a weed is to be seen anywhere (Fig. 117).   It would seem as if the constant care a Dutchman must bestow on his land, to protect it from

Fig. 116.—Dutch Garden, 1653.

destruction, and "make" the earth fit for produce, induces him to think all nature requires his improving hand ; hence the trees are mercilessly trimmed and cut, and the stranger in Haarlem is amused with the square and oblong masses of foliage which appear so compact upon the summits of the poles in front of the houses (Fig. 118).   These stems of the tortured plants are sometimes further improved (and the stranger more completely mystified) by

being painted with the bright colours a Dutchman so delights in.
These town-trees are most frequently trained over an iron trellis-
work, to which each branch is affixed, like an espalier to an
orchard-wall, and every straggling shoot or leaf lopped away.
Sometimes, at a street corner, a naked stump supports a flat
screen of verdure, which faces each angle of the house like a fire-
screen (Fig. 119).   The trees most employed are the yew, the

Fig. 117.—A Modern Dutch Garden.

holly, and the box : here the patience of the gardener reaps a rich
reward, and in process of time he can torture them into any
form :—

> " The suffering eye inverted nature sees,—
> Trees cut to statues, statues thick as trees."

It would scarcely be imagined that so stolid a people as the
Dutch would be carried away by an enthusiasm for flowers.   Yet
the annals of their tulip-mania, in the seventeenth century, are

unequalled in the world. In 1635, the rage among the Dutch to possess them was so great, that the ordinary industry of the country was neglected, and the population, even to its lowest dregs, embarked in the tulip trade. As the mania increased prices augmented, until, in the year 1635, many persons were known to invest a fortune of 100,000 florins in the purchase of forty roots. One tulip, named Admiral Liefkin, was valued at

Fig. 118.—Dutch Tree.

4,400 florins ; the rarest, named Semper Augustus, at 5,500. At one period only two of these bulbs were in Holland, one at Amsterdam, the other at Haarlem ; for the latter, twelve acres of building ground was offered ; the former was purchased for 4,000 florins, and a carriage and horses. Munting, a Dutch writer of the day, has written a folio on the rage, which now took the form of gambling, and regular marts for tulip-sales were opened in all the principal towns of Holland ; but, though large purchases were effected at enormous prices, the tulips did not really make part of the transaction : they represented but a gambling medium, and ultimately the holders of the bulbs, who sold to realise their profits, found, when the *furore* had abated, that they represented no real property. Hundreds became ruined men, and it was many years before the country recovered from the miseries this gambling in flowers had produced.

By the aid of these notes and sketches we hope to have made

Fig. 119.—Dutch Tree.

Holland better known to Englishmen. It is a country whose quaint peculiarities have no semblance elsewhere. Its features are unique, its people highly national ; its history one of the most exciting and glorious that can be offered to the student or the patriot. In its connection with the development of the great Reformation in the Church, or with the politics of our own country, it abounds in interest ; and it is somewhat singular that a country which offers so much to attract the attention of the educated tourist should be so little visited.

We now bid adieu to the Dutch painters. In the course of our remarks we have enforced the nature of their peculiar claims, and we need not here recount them. No school was more *realistic* in its tendencies, none honester in its truthful delineation of nature, or more capable of evolving the poetry in ordinary life. Spite of all prejudice they worked the mine well which they knew contained the gold, and though some of the dross may adhere to the metal, the gold is there in its native purity also.

THE HOUSE OF MICHAEL ANGELO,
AT FLORENCE.

THE HOUSE OF MICHAEL ANGELO, AT FLORENCE.

HERO-WORSHIP is natural to all men, and the most anti-poetic have their heroes, whom they worship all unconsciously themselves, while laughing at the enthusiasm of more poetic minds. The constructor of the most matter-of-fact piece of machinery has some other machinist in his mind's eye, to whom he looks up with the reverence, not unmixed with the awe, belonging to a superior. All this is but another phase in the mental homage paid from man to man when the mind of each is attuned to the same study, and can therefore best appreciate triumphs attained by the earnest thought of his fellow. The man who studies a steam-engine, and he who dreams over a picture by Turner, are both similarly occupied in hero-worshipping; their heroes only are different.

Coleridge, who spent a life in day-dreams, had a particular objection to that off-shoot of hero-worship, which invests with a sacred interest all that connects itself with the worldly presence of the hero; and he consequently argued against the custom of visiting localities sanctified by the residence of men of genius.

He held that it was a disenchantment, a destruction of previous imaginings, to go to a place and find it a very different thing to that you had built up in your own mind. But the same argument would hold good with regard to portraiture, and prevent us from thus studying our great authors, lest our notions of their features should be rudely destroyed. It is clear that the great majority of the world differs entirely from Coleridge, and desires to see memorials of the men, and the localities they lived in, as the best mode of realising their sojourn on earth.

Many weary miles have been trodden, and much peril and privation undergone, in thus wandering in the pathways of the great departed; but " the labour we delight in physics pain," and it may be doubted if happier moments are ever passed than those enjoyed by the enthusiastic man employed in such investigations. It has been my fortune to enjoy many, and to secure them I have travelled often out of my way for very long distances, always abundantly rewarded in the end; and never better than recently, when a run by rail from Leghorn to Florence gave me the chance of seeing the house of Michael Angelo, an art-hero worthy all worship. Let it be now my pleasant task to conduct the reader over this old mansion, and, by the aid of a few woodcuts, endeavour to give a true idea of its features to those who only "travel in books."

Some twenty years ago, when the last descendant of the great sculptor died in the person of the Minister of Public Instruction, the Cavalier Buonarotti, the Florentine Government secured the house known as the "casa Buonarotti" as public property. It had been in the possession of the family of Michael Angelo nearly three centuries; when they failed the mansion was bought by the modern townsmen. The house is substantially the same as when he inhabited it; but not nearly so much so as those who put faith in guide-books would be led to imagine. Thus the best of them

Fig. 120.—House of Michael Angelo.

informs us the house is preserved precisely as he left it, which is simply not true. When we speak of it as substantially the same, we allude to its external general features and the internal arrangement of the rooms, but modernisations appear in both: they have been "adapted" to the changes in manners during the long time which has elapsed since the sculptor's death, and hence the house has in a great degree become a "comfortable modern residence," rather than a mediæval home of somewhat gloomy security.

The external features of the mansion may be readily comprehended in the sketch (Fig. 120). It is a solid square of large size, as worthy the name of *palazzo* as any other in Florence. It stands in the Via Ghibellina, at the corner of the street known as the Via dei Marmi Sudici. The aspect of such houses gives at once an idea of well-arranged suites of rooms. In his old age Michael must have well appreciated his home, and it is easy in going over it to realise the great artist resting in his well-earned fame. The lowermost windows to the street are guarded, as all are in Italian towns, by strong external ironwork, giving it a somewhat prison-like look. A wide doorway leads through a passage to the inner open court of the house ; a door in the passage admits to the ground-floor apartments, now occupied by two tenants, one being an artist. Beside the artist's door, to the right, is the stair leading to the upper floors. The large range of windows in these floors are not all *real,* some few are blanks, and the whole have probably been altered during the last century from the irregular series which once covered the *façade.* The street in which the house stands is a wide and pleasant one ; it is on the quiet outskirts of the town ; the wall which encircles Florence is not many hundred yards from it ; and you see the picturesque hills around the glorious old city rise gradually above as you stand on the threshold of Michael's door. The palace of one of the old nobles faces the sculptor's house ; close beside it is another ; and the narrow street opposite, the Via della Pinzochere, leads direct to the great square and church of Santa Croce, whose windows and sculptured walls may be clearly seen from the same point of view.

The most original and unchanged "bit" of the house is the small court-yard (Fig. 121). Here the quaint construction of the building is most visible; the bracketed gallery, tall tower, and

Fig. 121.—Court-yard.

angular passages, with their narrow windows and bold defiance of symmetry, carry the mind back to the time when the sculptor inhabited it. The feeling is aided by the curious collection of fragments of antique sculpture inserted in the walls. Michael's love for Greek and Roman art was profound; he lived at a period when enthusiasm like his might be well indulged, and continually called forth by the discoveries then constantly making in Rome. In his time the finest antiquities were exhumed ; and those we look upon here are such as he could secure for himself. They are very varied in character and quality ; but they are valuable as showing how catholic his tastes were, and how much he respected all that

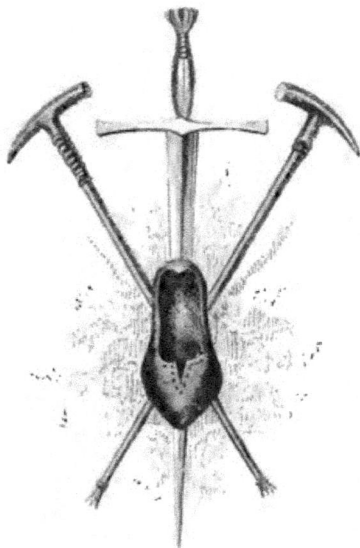

Fig. 122.—Group of Relics.

time had left us as aids to understand the life of past ages. Small as the collection is, it includes statues, *bassi-relievi*, funeral *cippi*, and inscriptions ; as well as a few early Christian inscriptions from the catacombs, noting, in the simple phraseology of the true faith, the last resting-places of " the just made perfect."

An arched staircase, somewhat steep, with a convenient

handrail beside it, leads to the suite of rooms on the first floor ; these are the rooms to which the public are admitted every Thursday. They are stately in their proportions, and communicate freely with each other. The first contains a large glass case filled with antique fragments, collected by Michael Angelo, with additions by the Cavalier Buonarotti, his ultimate representative. Fragments of sculpture, specimens of Greek and Roman cinerary urns, small *bassi-relievi*, and a host of minor articles, are here ; it is, in fact, such a collection as a man of classic taste would desire. On the walls are a few sketches, and here is hung the cross-hilted sword worn by Michael himself (Fig. 122) ; the handle is of steel, the grip covered with plated wire to give a firmer hold ; it is a good characteristic relic of the days when swords were essential, as well to indicate as to protect a gentleman. We pass from this into a capacious chamber, and thence into a long saloon at the angle of the house, lighted by two windows, between them a sedent statue of the sculptor by Antonio Novelli (Fig. 123). It is a good figure badly placed, with cross lights, or no lights at all— one of the sacrifices of art to expediency we are often condemned to feel. The walls and ceiling of this room are panelled, and the panels are pictured with scenes of the principal events of the sculptor's life, by Cristoforo Allori, Beliverti, Jacopo da Empoli, and Matteo Rosselli. Smaller compartments in *chiaro-oscuro* continue the series of minor events in the artist's history, and occupy their place beneath the larger coloured pictures. The ceiling is panelled into fifteen compartments, and here again are other delineations of the same kind. They are generally

admirably done, and most gratifying for the noble feeling they
exhibit of modern art-reverence towards its past professors.
English artists seem to feel little or no love for the great who
have gone before; and it is rarely that they paint incidents in the
lives of men of their own profession, though many smaller scenes

Fig. 123.—Saloon.

from the pages of Pepys and Boswell, or the pure inventions of
the novelist, are so immortalised. The continental painters, on the
contrary, most frequently select scenes from art-biography, and
some of their most successful works have resulted from that source.
The number of pictures in this chamber, and their power as works

of historic value, show that in the comparatively quiet life of an artist there is abundant scope for imaginative genius to work in.

In this room is a large oil painting by Michael Angelo; it is a "Holy Family," one of the very few works of its class that can be with certainty ascribed to him, exhibiting his powers and defects

Fig. 124.—Writing-Closet.

in about equal degrees. It has his grandeur of conception, with occasional faulty drawing, and decidedly bad colour; the latter a defect visible in all his works. A door on each side of this picture conducts to a square chamber, with a richly-panelled ceiling; the walls covered by presses of oak, containing folios of sketches by Angelo, among them that for his celebrated fresco "The Last

Judgment," and various personal relics. In the passage to this chamber are placed two busts and a boldly sculptured arm ;—all antique works of the Roman era which were found in the studio of Michael at Rome, and removed thence after his decease. The most interesting memorials are kept in a small closet in this apartment, which was used by the sculptor for writing in (Fig. 124). A railed escritoire so completely crowds this *sanctum* that it admits but a small seat in front. In the escritoire is kept one of the slippers he used to wear: it was laced up the front, is of roomy proportion, as will be seen in our cut (Fig. 122). Upon the wall above are hung the crutch-sticks he used in walking. The streets of Florence are flagged like those of ancient Italy, in large irregular flags of stone, and in wet weather afford an uncertain hold; consequently both these sticks have been furnished with ferrules cut into points to give greater security on the slippery pavement. Our group of relics exhibits both these sticks (Fig. 122). The other rooms contain some few specimens of old furniture, and we engrave an example of the chairs (Fig. 125). The walls are covered with sketches by Michael Angelo; some will at once be recognised as the originals from which Ottley copied the examples in his work on Italian Art, particularly the fine head of " Cleopatra," and a " Madonna and Child." Here is also the altar-piece, in low relief, after the manner of Donatello, in which Angelo gave another conception of the Madonna ; and a copy of it in bronze attributed to John of Bologna. The same artist's bust of Michael Angelo is in the last apartment of the suite.

We will leave the house, and pass up the narrow street opposite to the church of Santa Croce—aptly and justly styled "The Westminster Abbey of Florence"—for so short a distance is it to the sculptor's grave. In the nave of the solemn building, among the great and good of the past, who have made Florence famous, rests the aged sculptor. His tomb was erected some time after his

Fig. 125.—Specimen of Furniture.

decease; it is more ambitious than pleasing (Fig. 126). It is composed of coloured marbles; figures (life-size) of Poetry, Painting, and Architecture, are seated at the base of a sarcophagus, which is surmounted by Lorenzi's bust of Michael Angelo. As if to afford a foil to a questionable work by an unquestionably worse one, the wall above and around it has been painted with drapery, and angels upholding it, in the worst style of fresco. This addition we have felt justified in omitting from our cut. The great ones of the earth, who have nothing but birth or title to be remembered by, may require elaborate monuments to secure them from oblivion; Genius asks but a plain stone, where the living heart

Fig. 120.—The Tomb.

of a true worshipper may beat more quickly with thoughtful love towards the clay beneath.

In rambling through the pleasant streets of Florence, encountering on all sides the finest art-workmanship of its palmiest days, we constantly feel the spiritual presence of Michael and his compeers. Rome itself does not call forth greater memories.

You gaze admiringly upon works of the widest renown, belonging to the best periods of art, and which have often been the very origin of new phases in its practice. You study them as Angelo did, and with him for your critical guide—for he was no niggard in his praises of fellow-artists, if these laudations were fairly earned. Many anecdotes of his impulsive ardour are on record; and he often spoke to a life-like statue as if it really lived. Thus to Donatello's " St. George " he cried, " March! " after he had been struck by its grand military bearing. This and other noble works are still in the niches where he contemplated them, and unprotected by aught but the reverence of the Florentine people. The grand old city is freely adorned with priceless sculpture, part of the art-history of the world; and all is free to the touch of the commonest hand, yet no instance of mischief done to any is on record. The natives have been so familiar with these works from childhood, that they are as household gods to them. Would that this reverence was as visible elsewhere, and iconoclasm as little known as in the ducal city of Florence! Our fellow-countrymen might often learn lessons of wisdom, good sense, and right feeling, with reference to art-works, from the conduct of the humble classes of foreigners, upon whom we are too apt to look down.

RAFFAELLE IN ROME.

RAFFAELLE IN ROME.

WE consecrate the memory of great men, and when the master-spirit has flown to Him who gave it, is it not pardonable—nay, laudable—that we treat reverently the relics of their sojourn here—that we make pilgrimages to the homes they once inhabited—that we endeavour, as best we may, to call up to the mind's eye the very habit and manner of the great souls long departed, and let the mind linger over their earthly haunts as if awaiting their presence again to revivify the scenes made sacred to us by such connection? There is, perhaps, no spot more abounding with associations of all kinds, to interest men of every civilised country, and induce many hundred pilgrimages, than those few miles of ground upon which stands Rome, that imperial ruin in a papal garb:—

> " We cannot tread upon it but we set
> Our foot upon some reverent history."

The mind is here overwhelmed by the crowding memories of the great events of bygone time; "centuries look down upon us" from the ruined Colosseum—from the ivy-clad masses of wall where once stood the palace of the emperors of the world. These arches record their victories and their triumphs. This dirty, ill-enclosed space, now named from the cows that rest upon it after dragging the rude carts of the peasantry into Rome, was once the Forum—the very focus of all that was great in the whole history of the old world :—

> " Still the eloquent air breathes—burns with Cicero."

On this small patch of ground occurred events which form the most cherished memorials of history. Around us on all sides are the crumbling mementoes of the great of old, whose presence stirred the nations. The very fragments—the shadows of a shade —of their past greatness have been sufficient to revivify the human mind after many ages of mental darkness ; and the long-buried works of the old Romans, in the palmy days of Michael Angelo and Raffaelle, quickened the genius of their great minds, guided their thoughts aright, and ultimately led to the purity and nobility of modern art.

The great revival of learning in the fifteenth century led the student back from the legendary history of the middle ages to the more ennobling study of the classic era ; and this acquaintance with the acts of the great led to the desire to possess more tangible relics of their period. Hence coins and medals were sought after, not merely as works by ancient hands, but as authentic records of their history, rendered the more valuable by their autograph character. Inscriptions were sought for the same reasons. Statues were untombed, and gazed at in wonder, for the truth and beauty of their proportions, as contrasted with the gaunt conventionalities of their own schools of sculpture. Men regarded these works as the productions of superior beings; but such contemplation resulted in elevating the minds of the students, and slowly, but surely, the long-lost arts broke in full radiance from the clouds which had so long obscured them.

It was in these great days of resuscitation that Raffaelle lived. The popes and the nobles vied with each other in obtaining the best works of ancient art, and liberally rewarded the discoverers.[*] Lorenzo de Medici, well distinguished as "the Magnificent," made his palace at Florence a museum of art, and liberally gave free access to all students who chose to come there. Michael Angelo was of the number who studied in the beautiful garden where the sculpture was located, and the great duke often spoke encouragingly to the young lad who laboured there so thoughtfully and so well. Words led to deeds, and it was not long afterwards that the duke adopted Michael as his *protégé*, gave him a room in his palace, and was the friend of him and his family,

---

[*] Felice de Fredis, who discovered in 1508 the celebrated group, the Laocoon, in the Baths of Titus, had bestowed on him in consequence, by the Pope Julius II., the lucrative gift of the tolls and customs received at the Gate of St. John Lateran—an ample fortune in itself. Michael Angelo, who was in Rome at the time, describes the excitement the event caused. By a happy omen had his godfathers named him *Felice*. The gift was so large that the Church of St. John importuned the succeeding pope to compound with him for its restoration; but he only gave it up for the noble place of Apostolic Secretary, which he enjoyed until his death in 1529. He lies buried in the left transept of the Church of the Ara Cœli. The inscription on his grave-slab is nearly obliterated. Is there no kind hand in Rome, the city of sculptors, to recut the few lines recording the name of one who did the world of art much service?

death only severing the tie. Many other artists had to thank the liberal duke for the use of his art-treasures, and Raffaelle was among the number. The Cardinal Bembo, one of the most enlightened men of that day, rivalled the hospitality of the Medici, and received Raffaelle into his palace as an honoured guest;—and are not the names of both noble men more nobly immortalised by such patronage?

The early life of Raffaelle was happily circumstanced. His father was himself an artist, who saw his son's great genius, and fostered it from the birth. The child's early life was passed in a lovely home, rendered cheerful by the practice of refined pleasures, the only labour known there being the cheerful toil that awaits the student of art. Of pleasant manners and agreeable looks, the boy-artist made friends everywhere, and the record of his whole life is a narration of the accession of new friends. In the Italian cities where he went for study he made warm friendships with the best and greatest in art and literature. It rarely falls to the lot of a biographer to narrate a life of such unvarying happiness as that of Raffaelle. Pleasant and profitable as this genial study and companionship would naturally be to the young painter, whose devotion to art never relaxed, and whose patrons increased with his years, greater triumphs awaited him in the imperial city itself; and hither, in 1508, he travelled at the request of Pope Julius II., to decorate the halls of the Vatican, the invitation having come through his uncle Bramante, the great architect, who enjoyed the patronage of that pontiff. The artist was now twenty-five years of age, and had already given evidence of his powers; he had the fullest scope for their exertion, and the remainder of his too short life was devoted to the glory of the church and its head in Rome.

Fig. 127.—Raffaelle's First Residence, Rome.

In the labyrinth of short streets that lead to the heart of the old city, opposite Hadrian's Bridge, is situated the house in which Raffaelle first resided (Fig. 127). It is in a narrow street, known

as the Via Coronari ; the tall houses close it in, so that the sun never
reaches the lower stories—a valuable arrangement where shade is
grateful, but which gives a gloomy and stifling look to Italian
towns.   The house is featureless, and might not be recognised but
for the nearly decayed *chiaro-oscuro* portrait of its great tenant,
which was painted by Carlo Maratti in 1705, when it was renovated
and partly rebuilt. The interest of this house, in connection with
Raffaelle, did not cease with his life : it was ceded at his wish to
the Church of St. Maria della Rotonda, after his death, by his
executor, Baldassare de Pescia, the Papal Secretary, that a chapel
might be endowed to the honour of the Virgin in that venerable
building, where prayers should be said for the repose of his soul.
At that time the house produced a rent of seventy crowns per
annum.   In the year 1581, at the desire of Siticella, arch-priest of
the Pantheon, Gregory XIII. united the property to the revenue
of his office ; and in the year 1705, the arch-priest of that time
mortgaged the house to pay for the repairs noted above.   It now
produces a very small surplus, and that is said not to be applied to
the purposes indicated in the will.

The chief memorials of Raffaelle's residence in Rome are the
immortal works which still decorate the papal palace of the
Vatican.   The hall called *della Segnatura* was first decorated by
him with the great compositions known as "The Dispute of the
Sacrament," "The School of Athens," "The Parnassus," and
"Jurisprudence." They occupied him nearly three years. Toward
the end of that period the sight of Michael Angelo's grand conceptions in the Sistine Chapel are believed to have influenced the

young painter to a greater elevation in the treatment of his works. The sybils and prophets in the Church of Santa Maria della Pace, as well as the painting of the prophet Isaiah in the Church of St. Augustin, executed about this time, are cited as proofs of this influence. On the walls of the palace of Agostino Chigi he had painted his famous "Galatæa," and had achieved for himself a fixed and honourable position in Rome, surrounded by friends of the highest and most influential kind, and some few scholars who aided his labours.

In 1512 the second hall of the Vatican was commenced; in the February of the following year the pope died. Julius was more of a soldier than a churchman; and is recorded to have told Michael Angelo to place a sword rather than a book in the hand of the bronze statue he destined to commemorate him. Leo X. had more refined taste, and became celebrated as a patron of the arts. To narrate all Raffaelle's labours for this pontiff would be to give a list of renowned works, familiar to the whole world for their lessons of beauty, cultivated by the highest tech- nicalities of art. Suffice it to say that the art-labours of the Vatican never ceased, and when Bramante died Raffaelle was appointed his successor. His first architectural work was the rows of galleries which surround the court-yard of the Vatican, the foundations of which had only been laid by his uncle Bramante. These triple arcades rising above each other, and commanding magnificent views over Rome, were richly decorated by Raffaelle with designs which startled the world by their novelty and captivated by their beauty. Founded on the antique mural decorations then recently discovered in the Baths of Titus, the genius of the painter adopted their leading ideas, infusing the composition with his own fancy and grace, and thus gave a new decorative art to the world. Raffaelle was ever alive to the progress of art, and its interests were consulted by him in the largest way. He fostered the genius of Marc Antonio Raimondi, the engraver, at a period when the graphic art was in its infancy; in the midst of his laborious occupations he found time to design for him subjects for his *burin*, and to superintend their execution. But more than all, he defrayed the whole expenses of these engravings himself, taking Marc Antonio under his protection until the new art had established itself in popular favour, and could be followed as a lucrative profession. To Raffaelle, therefore, the art of engraving and the traders in prints owe a deep debt.*

The early artists were men of multifarious accomplishments; they were not painters only. We have record of their power in many branches, and examples of their versatility still remain to us; hence we need feel no surprise that the painter Raffaelle was installed to the post of papal architect. Michael Angelo also

---

* It should be noted, however, that Albert Dürer was really the chief populariser of the art. His prints on copper and wood (the latter particularly) had circulated over Northern Europe, and were well known in Venice. Raffaelle saw at once the latent power by means of which he might propagate and perpetuate his own designs, and at once encouraged the labours of Marc Antonio. This engraver had copied in Venice many of Dürer's engravings to his detriment, and Dürer had complained to the magistracy for redress. It is to Dürer we owe the discovery of etching and corroding a plate by acid, one of the greatest boons to the engraver, and an enormous saving of labour.

practised architecture, as well as sculpture and painting ; but more than this, he fortified the city of Florence, and successfully superintended its military defence during six months, when it was attacked by the Prince of Orange in 1529. Benvenuto Cellini has also left record of his fighting powers, when he served in the siege of the Castle of St. Angelo, in 1528. Albert Dürer introduced the Italian style of fortification to his native city of Nürnberg, and wrote a treatise on the art ; he was also painter, sculptor, designer, and engraver on wood, copper, and stone. Leonardo da Vinci excelled in the arts, and added thereto such sound philosophical views as to have been greatly in advance of his age ; indeed, his research in optical science has led to his being considered the father of the modern daguerreotype and photography, inasmuch as he propounded the possibility of securing images by the action of light alone.

Of Raffaelle's architectural powers Rome has varied examples. The principal are at the Vatican and St. Peter's, the construction of which he superintended during the rest of his brief life. On the authority of Vasari we may attribute to him one of the most beautiful of the Roman *palazzi*, the Villa Madama. The Caffarelli Palace is also known to be his design,* as well as the very beautiful funeral chapel for his friend and early patron Agostino Chigi, in the Church of Santa Maria del Popolo. Among the quiet gardens of the Celian Hill is one of his most picturesque

---

* It is opposite the Church of St. Andrea della Valle, and is now called the Palazzo Vidoni ; the upper portion is not Raffaelle's work.

works, the little Church of Santa Maria in Navicella, an edifice abounding with the most interesting artistic associations. It stands on the site of the house of one of the earliest Christian saints, St. Cyiac, and was built by Leo X. entirely from Raffaelle's design, with the exception of the simple and elegant little portico, which is by Michael Angelo. The paintings within are by Raf-

Fig. 128.—The Church of St. Maria in Navicella.

faelle's favourite scholars, Julio Romano and Pierino della Vaga. This interesting church takes its distinguishing name from the marble galley placed on a pedestal in front of the portico, by Pope Leo X., in whose time it was discovered. It is a curious work of the Roman era, and is seen in our cut with other classic fragments placed beside it (Fig. 128).

Raffaelle had now achieved so high a position in Rome, and

was so overwhelmed with commissions, that his scholars and assistants increased greatly. But for their aid it would have been impossible for him to have executed so large a number of works. It became his practice to design, superintend, and finish only; but the labour of carrying out his works was left to his scholars, who all became men of mark. The chief was Julio Romano, who painted a large portion of the Vatican. The Loggie was the work of many hands; the figures, the flowers, the scrolls, and the ornament, were all apportioned to the facile and ready powers of the army of artists the "divine master" had at command. It is recorded that he had a retinue of some fifty who were thus employed; these formed his train in public, so that "he appeared like a prince rather than an artist;" the fascination of his manners led to affection for himself irrespective of his genius.

But death came to carry the artist away in the midst of his triumph, ere he had entirely reaped the full harvest of his fame, leaving the world greatly the loser. Raffaelle, now a wealthy man, and living like a noble, had purchased for himself a mansion worthy of a nobleman born. His affianced bride, the niece of Cardinal Bibiena, died in 1518, and was buried in the Pantheon; and in April, 1520, the painter was laid in the same edifice (Fig. 129). It was less than twelve years of thought and action that had sufficed him to found immortal renown in Rome, and leave that city the bequest of the most glorious art-treasures in the world. His life had indeed been sacrificed to his eagerness to serve the pope. harassed by a multiplicity of engagements, Raffaelle had hurried from the Farnesina, the palace of the wealthy banker Chigi, which he was engaged to decorate, to consult with the pope about his works at the Vatican. He had overheated himself with running this quarter of a mile, and he felt a sudden chill as he stood in the cold unfinished building. He went to his palace (a short distance only), and in the course of a few days died there at the early age of thirty-seven, April 7th, 1520.

Fig. 129.—The Pantheon, Rome.

The last home of Raffaelle is still pointed out in Rome (Fig. 130). It stands in the district termed the Trastavere, in the small square midway from the Castle of St. Angelo and St. Peter's. It occupies one side of this square, and is an imposing structure. The architects were Bramante and Baldassare Peruzzi. It is now known as the Palazzo degli Convertiti, and devoted to the reception of converted heretics. Here his body lay in state in front of his unfinished picture of the "Transfiguration,"* his greatest, as it was his last, work. There was a grandeur in such a death—a glory in such a death-chamber, "which time has not yet effaced from the memory of man. It was one of those *impromptus* of the

Fig. 130.—Raffaelle's Last Residence, Rome.

eloquence of things which owed its effects to a cause so much the more active and fruitful, because it was natural and not arranged."†

——" And when all beheld
Him, where he lay, how changed from yesterday—

---

* The picture was afterwards finished by his pupil Julio Romano. It had been ordered by the Cardinal Medici for Narbonne, but was placed over the high altar of the Church of St. Pietro in Martorio, at Rome. It was then removed to the Vatican, from whence it was carried by Napoleon to Paris, but was restored to Rome at his fall.

† Quatremere de Quincy.

> Him in that hour cut off, and at his head
> His last great work ; when, entering in, they looked
> Now on the dead, then on the master-piece ;
> Now on his face, lifeless and colourless,
> Then on those forms divine that lived and breathed,
> And would live on for ages—all were moved ;
> And sighs burst forth, and loudest lamentation." *

All Rome mourned the death of the great painter. The pope wept bitter tears ; his loss was indeed great, for the spirit that could make his pontificate glorious had departed, and left none to fill the void. "Rome seems no longer Rome since my poor Raffaelle is gone," writes Castiglione to the marchioness his mother. His funeral *cortége* included in its ranks the greatest men in station, and the most talented in art and literature. These, with his friends and pupils, marched amid the lamentations of the whole city to the Pantheon, and reverently laid the painter beside the altar he had endowed.

Rome—perhaps the world—possesses no building of more interest than this. The ancients described it with admiration eighteen centuries ago, and it still remains the best preserved monument of modern Rome.

> "Relic of nobler days, and noblest arts !
> Despoil'd, yet perfect, with thy circle spreads
> A holiness appealing to all hearts—
> To art a model ; and to him who treads
> Rome for the sake of ages, Glory sheds
> Her light through thy sole aperture ; to those
> Who worship, here are altars for their heads ;

* Rogers's " Italy."

And they who feel for genius may repose
Their eyes on honour'd forms, whose busts around them close."*

Let us enter this noble relic of the past, sacred with the associations of ages. Over the portico is an inscription, recording

Fig. 131.—Raffaelle's Chapel.

its erection by Agrippa in his third consulate (B.C. 25); the pillars of this "more than faultless" portico are Corinthian columns of oriental granite. The bronze doors are antique; so is the open

---

* Byron, "Childe Harold's Pilgrimage." The busts are now all removed.

grating above them. You pass them, and the interior strikes you
at once by its simple grandeur. It is a rotunda supporting a
dome, the only light being received through the circular opening
in its centre. The rain falls freely upon the floor; and in the
pavement may be noted the star-shaped apertures by which it
may descend to the drains beneath. No antique building exists for
modern uses so unaltered as this.* In the walls are seven large
niches, and between them are eight *ædicula*, or shrines which have
been converted into altars. Opposite the entrance, to the left of
the centre, the visitor will notice an altar, in front of which hangs
a triple light, supported by a silver monogram of the Virgin;
the same monogram is above the altar (Fig. 131). It is that
founded by Raffaelle, for the perpetual support of which he gave
the house which forms the first of our engravings. The figure of the
Virgin and Child, now known as "La Madonna del Sasso," was
sculptured by his pupil Lorenzo Lotti. Under this altar the body
of Raffaelle was laid, and upon a lower panel of marble to the left
of it is the epitaph to the painter written by Cardinal Bembo. On
the opposite side is the epitaph to Annibale Caracci; and in other

---

* "Though plundered of all its brass, except the ring which was necessary to preserve
the aperture above—though exposed to repeated fire—though sometimes flooded by the river,
and always open to the rain—no monument of equal antiquity is so well preserved as this
rotunda. It passed with little alteration from the pagan into the present worship; and so
convenient were its niches for the Christian altars, that Michael Angelo, ever studious of
ancient beauty, introduced their design as a model in the Catholic Church."—FORSYTH'S
Italy. The bronze here alluded to, which once covered the interior of the dome, was stripped
off by Pope Urban VIII., and moulded into the great canopy now over the tomb of St. Peter
in Rome; the rest was used for cannon, which were placed on the Castle of St. Angelo.
Venuti has computed its weight at 450,250 lbs.

parts of the building are buried Raffaelle's betrothed wife, and his scholars, Giouanni da Udine and Perino della Vaga. Baldassare Peruzzi, one of the architects of Raffaelle's palace, also lies here ; as well as Taddeo Zuccari, and other eminent painters. Its most modern artistic monument is Thorwaldsen's bust to Cardinal Gonsalvi. Where can the art-pilgrim pay a more soul-inspiriting visit than to this

> " ———— sanctuary and home
> Of art and piety ? "

Carlo Maratti desired to place a more striking memorial of Raffaelle's resting place than the simple inscription, and accordingly, in the year 1674, a marble bust of the painter, executed by Paolo Nardini, was placed in one of the oval niches on each side of the chapel. The epitaph to Maria Bibiena (Raffaelle's betrothed) was removed to make way for Maratti's new inscription ; and it was currently believed that the skull of Raffaelle was removed ; at least such was the history given of a skull shown as the painter's, religiously preserved by the Academy of St. Luke, and descanted on by phrenologists as indicative of all the qualities which " the divine painter" possessed. But scepticism played its part : doubts of the truth of this story led to doubts of Vasari's statement respecting the exact locality of Raffaelle's tomb. Matters were brought to a final issue by the discovery of a document proving this skull to be that of Don Desiderio de Adjutorio, founder of the society called the Virtuosi, in 1542. Thereupon, this society demanded the head of its founder from the Academy of St. Luke ; but they would neither abandon that nor the illusion that they possessed the veritable skull of the great artist. Arguments ran high, and it was at length determined to settle the question by an examination of the spot, which took place on the 13th of September, 1833, in the presence of the Academies of St. Luke and of Archæology, the commission of the fine arts (including Overbeck and others), the members of the Virtuosi, the governor of Rome (Monsignor Grimaldi), and the Cardinal Zurla, the representative of the pope.

The result will be best given in the words of an eye-witness, Signor Nibby (one of the commission of antiquities and fine arts), who thus described the whole to M. Quatremere de Quincy, the biographer of Raffaelle:—"The operations were conducted on such a principle of exact method as to be almost chargeable with over-nicety. After various ineffectual attempts in other directions, we at length began to dig under the altar of the Virgin itself, and, taking as a guide the indications furnished by Vasari, we at length came to some masonry of the length of a man's body. The labourers raised the stone with the utmost care, and having dug within for about a foot and a half came to a void space. You can hardly conceive the enthusiasm of us all, when by a final effort the workmen exhibited to our view the remains of a coffin with an entire skeleton in it, lying thus as originally placed, and thinly covered with damp dust. We saw at once quite clearly that the tomb had never been opened, and it thus became manifest that the skull possessed by the Academy of St. Luke was not that of Raffaelle. Our first care was by gentle degrees to remove from the body the dust which covered it, and which we religiously collected, with the purpose of placing in it a new sarcophagus. Amongst it we found, in tolerable preservation, pieces of the coffin, which was made of deal, fragments of a painting which had ornamented the lid, several bits of Tiber clay formations from the water of the river, which had penetrated into the coffin by infiltration,* an iron *stelletta*, a sort of spur with which Raffaelle had been decorated by Leo X., several *fibulæ*, and a number of

Fig. 132.—The Grave of Raffaelle.

metal *anelli*, portions of his dress." These small rings had fastened the shroud; several were retained by the sculptor Fabris, who also took casts of the head and hand, and Camuccini took

---

* This will be understood when we remember that the Tiber has inundated this lower part of Rome several times. On the external wall of the adjoining Church of Santa Maria sopra Minerva, are the marks of the height to which the waters rose, and which is five feet above the pavement level.

views of the tomb and its precious contents. From one of these our cut is copied.

On the following day the body was further examined by professional men; the skeleton was found to measure five feet seven inches; the narrowness of the coffin indicated a slender and delicate frame. This accords with the contemporary accounts, which say he "was of a refined and delicate constitution; his frame was all spirit; his physical strength so limited that it was a wonder he existed so long as he did." The investigation completed, the body was exhibited to the public from the 20th to the 24th, and then was again placed in a new coffin of lead, and that in a marble sarcophagus presented by the pope, and taken from the antiquities in the Museum of the Vatican. A solemn mass was then announced for the evening of the 18th of October. The Pantheon was illuminated, as for a funeral; "the sarcophagus, with its contents, was placed in exactly the same spot whence the remains had been taken. The presidents of the various academies were present, with the Cavalier Fabris at their head. Each bore a brick, which he inserted in the brickwork with which the sepulchre was walled in." And so the painter awaits "the resurrection of the just," and the fellowship of saints and angels, of which his inspired pencil has given us the highest realisation on earth.

THE END.

PRINTED BY VIRTUE AND CO., CITY ROAD, LONDON.

www.ingramcontent.com/pod-product-compliance
Lightning Source LLC
Chambersburg PA
CBHW030343270326
41926CB00009B/945